SWEATERS
FROM THE SEATON COLLECTION

More than 20 Innovative Pullovers, Cardigans, Vests, and Jackets to Knit

BY JAMIE AND JESSI SEATON • PHOTOGRAPHS BY FRANK HERHOLDT

Clarkson N. Potter, Inc./Publishers

For Douglas Ronald Seaton

Text and original design copyright © Jamie and Jessi Seaton 1989
Photographs copyright © 1989 by Frank Herholdt

Published in the United States of America by Clarkson N. Potter, Inc.,
225 Park Avenue South, New York, New York 10003
and distributed by Crown Publishers, Inc., New York

Published in Great Britain by Century Hutchinson Ltd.

Clarkson N. Potter, Potter, and colophon are trademarks
of Clarkson N. Potter, Inc.

Manufactured in Singapore

Library of Congress Cataloging-in-Publication Data

Seaton, Jamie.
Sweaters from the Seaton Collection: 25 innovative pullovers,
cardigans, and vests to knit / by Jamie and Jessi Seaton;
photographs by Frank Herholdt.
p.   cm.
ISBN 0-517-57225-7: $24.95
1. Knitting—Patterns.   2. Sweaters.   I. Seaton, Jessi.
II. Title.
TT825.S43   1989
746.9'2—dc19   88-38430
CIP
10 9 8 7 6 5 4 3 2 1

First American Edition

CONTENTS

*Are available as kits in retail shops stocking Rowan Yarns. For UK and overseas stockists, see page 143. †Are available as kits by mail order only from Ehrman. For UK and overseas stockists, see page 143. The rest of the designs are available as kits by mail order only from the Seatons, see page 143.

INTRODUCTION

I've been designing knitwear for ten years now, and this book contains the very best of what we've produced in that time. After a decade of working season in and season out, devising and making two new collections a year, it has been very satisfying to take the time to have a long look at what we have done, and to choose what we think is the best. It is satisfying, too, to see these designs freshly made up, recoloured and restyled as necessary to form what has turned out to be a cogent collection in its own right, and to see them so beautifully photographed and presented.

Although there was ten years' work to choose from, all but one of these designs, in fact, date from the last three years. I hope that, to some extent, this indicates that the longer I do this work, the better the work I do! But it also reflects a more general trend, namely, the immeasurable improvement in the technical standard of home knitting since the mid-seventies. People are far more willing to experiment, and to take on projects that at first sight look dauntingly difficult; and ninety-nine times out of a hundred they succeed magnificently. This gives me a much freer hand to design garments just as I want them to be, with far less need to consider the restrictions that are imposed by limited technical skills. Ten years ago I might have been rather pushing my luck if I had designed a sweater with more than three colours in a row, whereas now I am freshly amazed every new season by our knitters' ability to take in their stride whatever technical difficulties we present them with.

It would be misleading to describe these designs as 'easy-knits'; but they are really not as difficult as one might imagine them to be at a glance. When we take on new knitters they often find the first piece of the first garment rather slow going; but having surmounted that initial hurdle they get into the feel of the pattern, and often become addicted to this kind of knitting – no chunky-knit, mohair pullover will ever be satisfying again! So, although making these garments does require time and concentration, it's well worth persevering; the process itself is rewarding and enjoyable, and at the end you have a stylish, good-looking garment that is also practical, easy-to-wear and adaptable.

There has always been a tradition of skilled, fine-quality knitting in Britain – look at the wonderful variety of fishermen's jerseys and genuine old Fair Isles. Somehow, in the fifties, sixties and early seventies that tradition was diminished by the onslaught of mass production, cheap acrylic yarns and the 'quick-knits' that were promoted by the knitting companies. It has been very pleasing and exciting to see the tradition coming back to life with renewed vigour and direction.

All the designs in this book are made using the intarsia technique of working with colours (see page *141*). This isn't difficult to master at all; if you can knit stocking stitch, intarsia is only a small step away; and if you can knit intarsia, the world of multi-coloured pattern is your oyster! Loving colour and varied patterning as I do, it really is *the* knitting technique for me. It allows me to design pieces with as much or as little pattern as I like, to use as many colours as I like, to work a regular, repeating pattern or an irregular, non-repeating one on as small or as large a scale as I please; and it still always gives a light, elastic, even-tensioned fabric. With the Fair Isle technique, on the other hand, one is restricted to repeating patterns – and even then, if you use more than three colours in a row, you might well end up with a stiff, inflexible fabric that will quite likely felt up the first time you wash it!

I generally use fairly lightweight yarns – four-ply or double knitting. It might take longer to knit the garment, but the delicacy and detail of pattern and the lightness of touch that you can achieve with fine yarn makes it well worth it. Also, I tend to think

The patchwork blanket shown here is made up of try-out swatches. These accumulate over the seasons, allowing us the bonus of piecing together one of these blankets every couple of years or so. This is a very satisfying job, concentrating a record of some years' work into one item.

that the thicker the yarn the harder it is to achieve an elegant, graceful, wearable style. A good piece of knitwear should complement and flatter the shape of the body, rather than smother it beneath acres of heavyweight stitchery!

I use a lot of colours in my designs – usually between twelve and twenty in each, and it's often an effort to restrict myself to so few. I try to bear in mind that using a lot of colours isn't automatically a key to good design; sometimes an excess of colours serves only to dilute a mood that would come across more strongly if fewer, more carefully chosen ones were used. The choice of colours *is* very important. Bad colouring can ruin a good pattern; good colouring can rescue a mediocre one. Frequently, when working on colourways, I'm struck by the close equivalence between colour in pattern and notes in music; different colours will harmonize or clash with one another just as musical notes do, producing chords or dis-chords that suggest particular moods or feelings. I love playing around with colours, discovering the different ways they affect each other, finding tones and hues that produce new harmonies.

The design process is sometimes easy, sometimes difficult. There's really no key to good design, but it is important, firstly, to have a delight in what you're doing, in colour, nuance, rhythm and detail; and, secondly, to be as obstinate as hell, and to stick at what you're doing, no matter how long it takes or how many times you have to start again, until you've got it just right.

We photographed the garments in Tuscany in May. This was partly because my designs have such diverse influences that Renaissance Italy seemed one of the few places that would happily accommodate them. There you would be as likely to find a piece of Danish needlework as an Afghan embroidery, a Persian carpet as a French tapestry. But more than that, we thought the warm Italian light, and the atmosphere, in general, would complement these designs. This turned out to be true; the light brought the colours to such vivid life that I found myself looking at the garments as if for the first time. And the atmosphere, despite the prevailing rural calm and the relaxed, easy feel of the towns, somehow seemed to encourage, approve of and reward attempts at elegance or beauty.

I began by saying how satisfying it was to look back and assemble this collection. It's also satisfying, after ten years, to pass these designs on to the home knitter. Previously they have only been available from the shops we sell to, and then only at very high prices. Now they can be knitted in your own home, at your own pace, for your own pleasure and to your own satisfaction. I hope you enjoy them, both in the making and in the wearing.

Jamie Seaton.

This sweater was designed especially for an exhibition at Henri Bendel's in New York. The idea was to produce a one-off piece, where all the constraints normally imposed by production considerations could be ignored. Thus it could be as difficult to knit and could have as many colours as I liked – something I really enjoyed doing.

RENAISSANCE

*The main picture shows
Sicily (page 16) with
(from top left,
anticlockwise) the back of
the Nosegay waistcoat
(page 22), Diamonds
(page 31), Cherubs (page
10), and the back of the
Sicily cardigan in the black
colourway.*

CHERUBS

This is an oversized sweater which can even be worn as a mini-dress. I designed the pattern after a visit to Florence in 1987; it's typical of Roman and – rediscovered 1000 years later – Italian Renaissance wall decoration. Urns, cherubs, swags, flora and fauna all come into these designs, which are held together beautifully by sweeping, classical geometrics.

SIZES
To fit: 91[96,101]cm (36[38,40]in) bust
Actual width measurement: 109[114,119]cm (43[45,47]in)
Length: 66·5[68,69]cm (26¼[26¾,27¼]in)
Sleeve seam: 47[48,49·5]cm (18½[19,19½]in)

MATERIALS
600[600,625]g (22[22,23]oz) four-ply cotton in blue (A)
50g (2oz) each in pale beige (B), sky (C), pastel green (D), peacock (E) and blue-green (F)
25g (1oz) each in purple-grey (G), mid-grey (H), pale grey (J), maroon (L), gold (M), mulberry (N), mauve pink (Q) and clear blue-green (R)
1 pair each 2¼mm (US1) and 2¾mm (US2) needles

TENSION
31 sts and 43½ rows to 10cm (4in) over patt on 2¾mm (US2) needles.
Note: Work colour patt by the intarsia method, see page 141.

BACK
Using 2¼mm (US1) needles and yarn A, cast on 157[165,173] sts.
Work in twisted rib as foll:
1st row (rs) (K1 tbl, P1) to last st, K1 tbl.
2nd row (P1, K1 tbl) to last st, P1.
Rep these 2 rows 12 times more, then 1st row again.
Next row Rib 12[16,15], * make 1, rib 12[12,13]; rep from * ending last rep rib 13[17,15]. 169[177,185] sts.
Change to 2¾mm (US2) needles and work 2 rows in st st, beg with a K row.
Now beg colour patt from chart 1, working in st st throughout, as foll:
1st row (rs) K22[26,30]A, 3B, 5A, 3B, 103A (reversing chart after working centre st), 3B, 5A, 3B, 22[26,30]A.
2nd row P23[27,31]A, 3B, 4A, 2B, 51A, 3M, 51A, 2B, 4A, 3B, 23[27,31]A.
These two rows set position of chart 1 patt.
Cont as set until 158[160,162] rows have been worked from top of rib, end with a ws row.

Shape armholes
Cast off 5 sts at beg of next 2 rows.
159[167,175] sts. **
Now work straight until 254[260,264] rows have been worked from top of rib (when chart patt is complete, cont in A only).
Shape shoulders
Cast off 17[18,19] sts at beg of next 4 rows, then 18[19,20] sts at beg of foll 2 rows.
Leave rem 55[57,59] sts on a spare needle for neckband.

FRONT
Work as given for back to **.
Now work straight until 229[233,235] rows have been worked from top of rib, ending with a rs row.
Divide for neck
Next row Patt 73[76,79] sts and leave these sts on a spare needle, patt 13[15,17] sts and leave these sts on a stitch holder for neckband, patt to end. 73[76,79] sts.
Cont on these sts only for first side of neck.
Work 1 row.
Cast off 3 sts at beg of next and foll 4 alt rows, then dec 1 st at neck edge on next 6 rows. 52[55,58] sts.
Now work 10[12,14] rows straight, ending at armhole edge (256[262,266] rows have been worked from top of rib).
Shape shoulder
Cast off 17[18,19] sts at beg of next and foll alt row. 18[19,20] sts.
Work 1 row.
Cast off.
With rs of work facing rejoin yarn to sts left on spare needle and complete second side of neck to match first side reversing shapings.

SLEEVES
Using 2¼mm (US1) needles and yarn A, cast on 67[69,71] sts.
Work 39 rows in twisted rib as for back.
Next row Rib 2[3,4], * make 1, rib 2; rep from * ending last rep rib 3[4,5]. 99[101,103] sts.
Change to 2¾mm (US2) needles and beg colour patt from chart 2, reversing chart patt after working centre st, *at the same time* inc 1 st

CHERUBS CHART 1

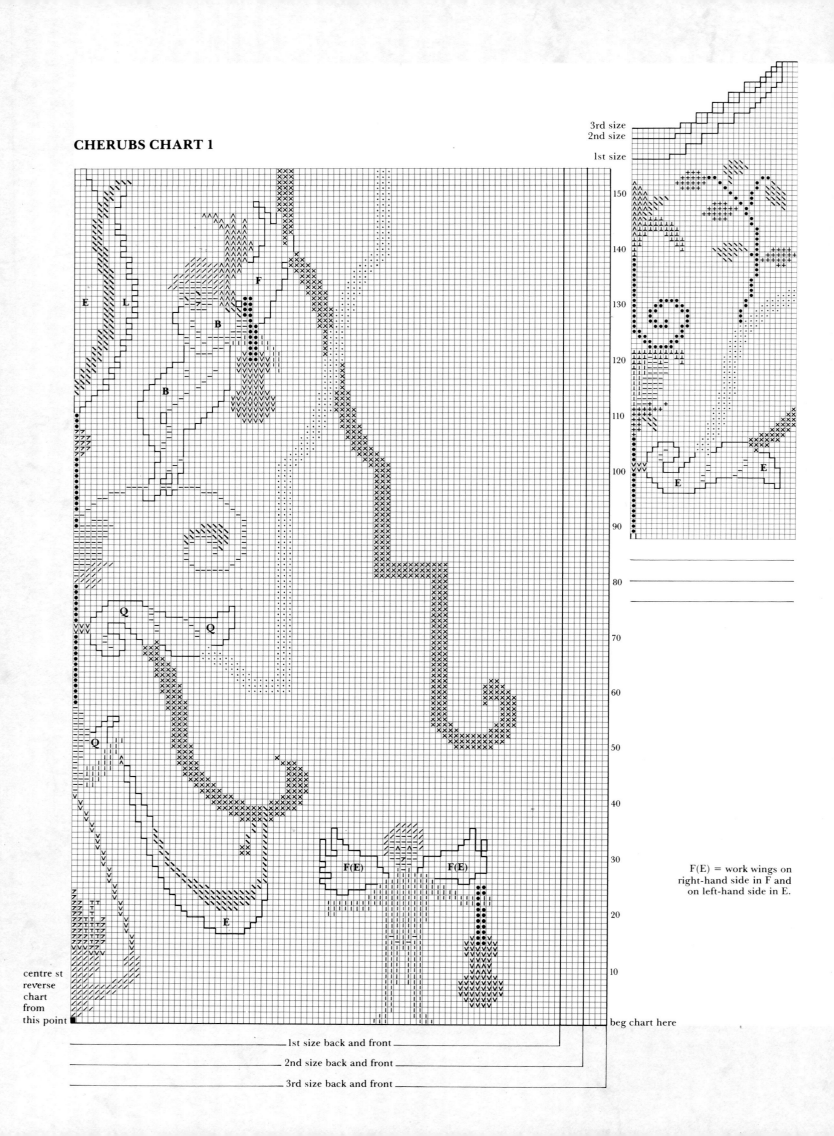

3rd size
2nd size

1st size

E   L

F

B

B

150

140

130

120

110

100

90

80

Q

Q

70

60

Q

50

40

F(E)   F(E)

30

E

20

10

centre st
reverse
chart
from
this point

beg chart here

F(E) = work wings on
right-hand side in F and
on left-hand side in E.

1st size back and front

2nd size back and front

3rd size back and front

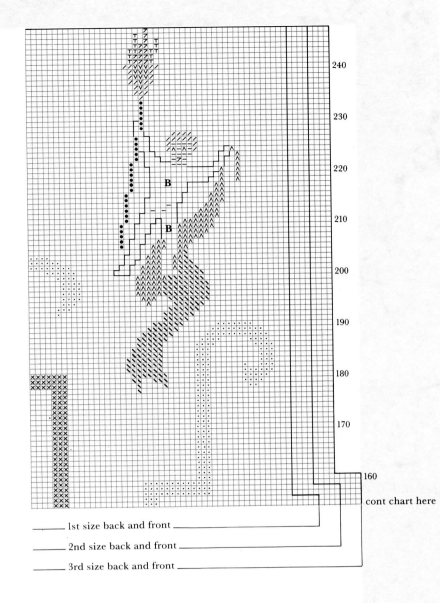

240

230

220

B

210

B

200

190

180

170

160

cont chart here

_____ 1st size back and front _____

_____ 2nd size back and front _____

_____ 3rd size back and front _____

☐ A unless
  otherwise
  indicated

⫞ B

⊠ C

⊡ D

◪ E

◩ F

▽ G

◉ H

⊟ J

◪ L

◪ M

⊓ N

⊡ Q

⊞ R

at each end of every foll 4th row until there are 165[171,175] sts (when chart patt is complete, cont in A only), ending with a ws row.
Work 22 rows straight.
Cast off.

COLLAR
Using 2¼mm (US1) needles and yarn A, cast on 140[146,152] sts.
Work in K1, P1 rib until collar measures 11cm (4½in).
Cast off loosely in rib.

TO MAKE UP
Join right shoulder seam.
Neckband
With rs of work facing, using 2¼mm (US1) needles and yarn A, K up 33[34,35] sts down left front neck, K13[15,17] sts from stitch holder at front neck, K up 33[34,35] sts up right front neck, and K55[57,59] sts from spare needle at back neck. 134[140,146] sts.
Work 10 rows in K1, P1 rib.
Cast off loosely in rib.
Join left shoulder and neckband seam.
Join on collar to inside of K-up edge of neckband, so that row-end edges meet neatly at centre front.
Set in sleeves, easing to fit around cast-off sts at underarm.
Join side and sleeve seams.

CHERUBS CHART 2

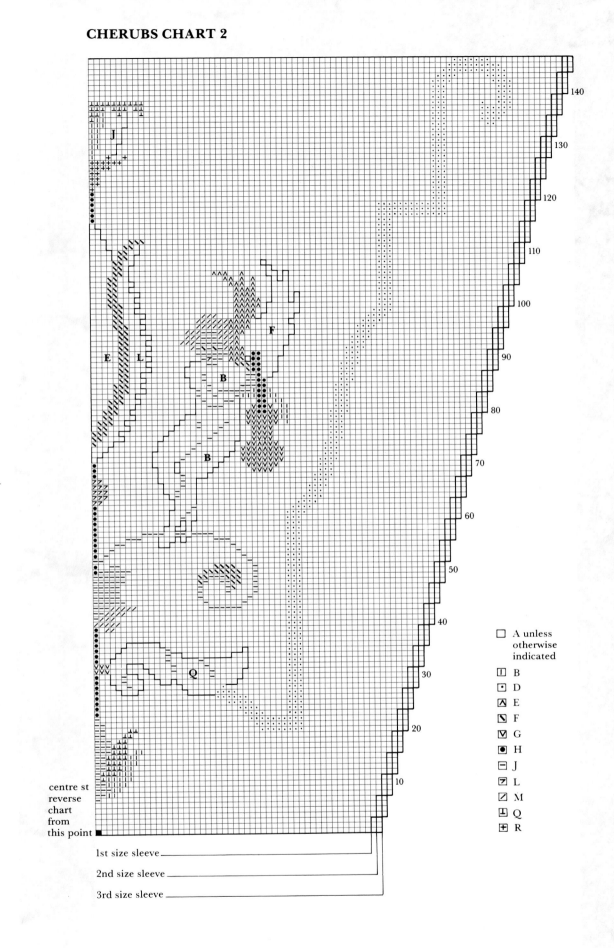

We photo-
graphed the
Cherubs
sweater in the
garden of a
villa in Lucca.
Abundant
greenery was
interspersed
with fountains,
ponds and neo-
classical
statuary – a
perfect setting.

SICILY

I particularly like this short, neat cardigan for the way pattern and shape and colour work so well together to produce a garment that, though quite understated and simple, is very wearable, elegant and flattering. The patterns were inspired by examples of seventeenth-century embroidery from Southern Italy and Sicily.

SIZES
To fit: 91[96,101]cm (36[38,40]in) bust
Actual width measurement: 106[111,116·5]cm (41¾[43¾,46]in)
Length: 50·5[51·5,53]cm (20[20¼,21]in)
Sleeve seam: 45[46,47]cm (17¾[18,18½]in)

MATERIALS
325[350,350]g (12[13,13]oz) four-ply wool in yellow (A)
50g (2oz) each in midnight blue (B), fuchsia (C), old rose (D) and blue mist (E)
25g (1oz) each in mulberry (F), lavender (G), magenta (H), dark blue (J), grey-green fleck (L), airforce (M), grey-blue (N) and cream (Q)
1 pair each 2¼mm (US1) and 2¾mm (US2) needles
7 buttons

TENSION
31 sts and 41 rows to 10cm (4in) over patt on 2¾mm (US2) needles.
Note: Work colour patt by the intarsia method, see page 141.

BACK
Using 2¼mm (US1) needles and yarn A, cast on 147[155,163] sts.
Work in twisted rib as foll:
1st row K1 tbl, * P1, K1 tbl; rep from * to end.
2nd row P1, * K1 tbl, P1; rep from * to end.
Rep these 2 rows 8 times more, then 1st row again.
Next row Rib 6[10,14], * make 1, rib 9; rep from * ending last rep rib 6[10,14]. 163[171, 179] sts.
Change to 2¾mm (US2) needles and beg colour patt from chart 1, work in st st, as foll:
1st-4th rows Work in st st in A, beg with a K row.
5th row K9[13,17]A, (17B, 15A) 4 times, 17B, 9[13,17]A.
6th row P9[13,17]A, (17B, 15A) 4 times, 17B, 9[13,17]A.
These 6 rows set position of chart patt.
Cont in this way, work to centre st, work centre st, then work row in reverse ending at right-hand edge of chart, until 86[88,92]

rows in all have been worked from chart 1, ending with a ws row.
Shape armholes
Cast off 5 sts at beg of next 2 rows.
153[161,169] sts.
Now work straight until chart 1 is completed.
Cont in A only, work 1[5,11] rows, ending with a ws row.
Shape shoulders
Cast off 17[18,19] sts at beg of next 4 rows, then 16[17,18] sts at beg of foll 2 rows.
Leave rem 53[55,57] sts on a spare needle.

LEFT FRONT
Using 2¼mm (US1) needles and yarn A, cast on 71[75,79] sts.
Work 19 rows in twisted rib as given for back.
Next row Rib 4[6,8], * make 1, rib 8; rep from * ending last rep rib 3[5,7]. 80[84,88] sts.
Change to 2¾mm (US2) needles and beg colour patt from chart 1, working in st st throughout, and K all odd-numbered rows, P all even-numbered rows, work 1st-80th rows (omitting ribbon motif from 72nd row onwards).
Now beg colour patt from chart 2, work 6[8,12] rows, ending at armhole edge.
Shape armhole
Cast off 5 sts at beg of next row. 75[79,83] sts. Now work 80 rows straight, ending at front opening edge.
Shape neck
Cast off 4 sts at beg of next row, then 3 sts at beg of 5 foll alt rows.
Now dec 1 st at neck edge on next 6[7,8] rows. 50[53,56] sts.
Work 8[9,10] rows straight (when chart 2 is completed, cont in A only), ending at armhole edge.
Shape shoulder
Cast off 17[18,19] sts at beg of next and foll alt row. 16[17,18] sts.
Work 1 row. Cast off.

RIGHT FRONT
Work as given for left front of cardigan, reversing 1st-80th rows of chart 1, chart 2, and all shapings.

I coloured the cardigan this way especially for the book — a lovely sophisticated Chinese yellow, warm and sunny without being garish. For contrast colours I've used mostly a silk and wool mixture to add some texture to the fabric.

SICILY CHART 1

180

170

160

150

140

130

120

110

100

90

80

70

60

50

40

30

20

10

centre st
reverse
chart
from
this point

——— 1st size back and front ———

——— 2nd size back and front ———

——— 3rd size back and front ———

☐	A
◩	B
⊞	C
◧	D
⊡	E
⫿	F
◪	G
◸	H
◮	J
⊙	L
⊤	M
⊠	N
⊟	Q

SICILY CHART 2

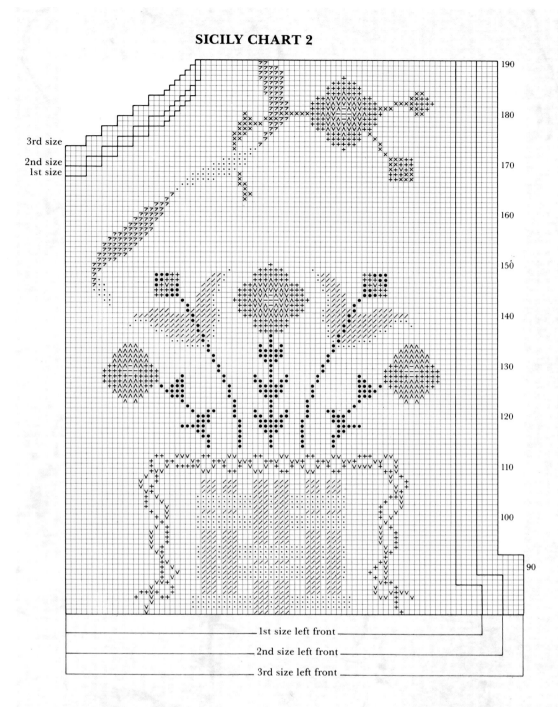

3rd size
2nd size
1st size

1st size left front
2nd size left front
3rd size left front

SLEEVES

Using 2¼mm (US1) needles and yarn A, cast on 69[71,73] sts.

Work 23 rows in twisted rib as for back.

Next row Rib 4[6,6], * make 1, rib 3; rep from * end last rep rib 5[5,7]. 90[92,94] sts.

Change to 2¾mm (US2) needles and beg colour patt from chart 3, working in st st throughout, *at the same time* inc 1 st at each end of every foll 3rd row until there are 176[180,184] sts (129[132,135] rows have been worked from chart).

Work 35[36,37] rows straight (when chart 3 is complete cont in A only). Cast off.

BUTTON BAND

With rs of work facing, using 2¼mm (US1) needles and yarn A, K up 158[160,162] sts evenly down left front edge from beg of neck shaping to cast-on edge.

Work 10 rows in K1, P1 rib.

Cast off in rib.

BUTTONHOLE BAND

With rs of work facing, using 2¼mm (US1) needles and yarn A, K up 158[160,162] sts up right front edge from cast-on edge to beg of neck shaping.

Work 4 rows in K1, P1 rib.

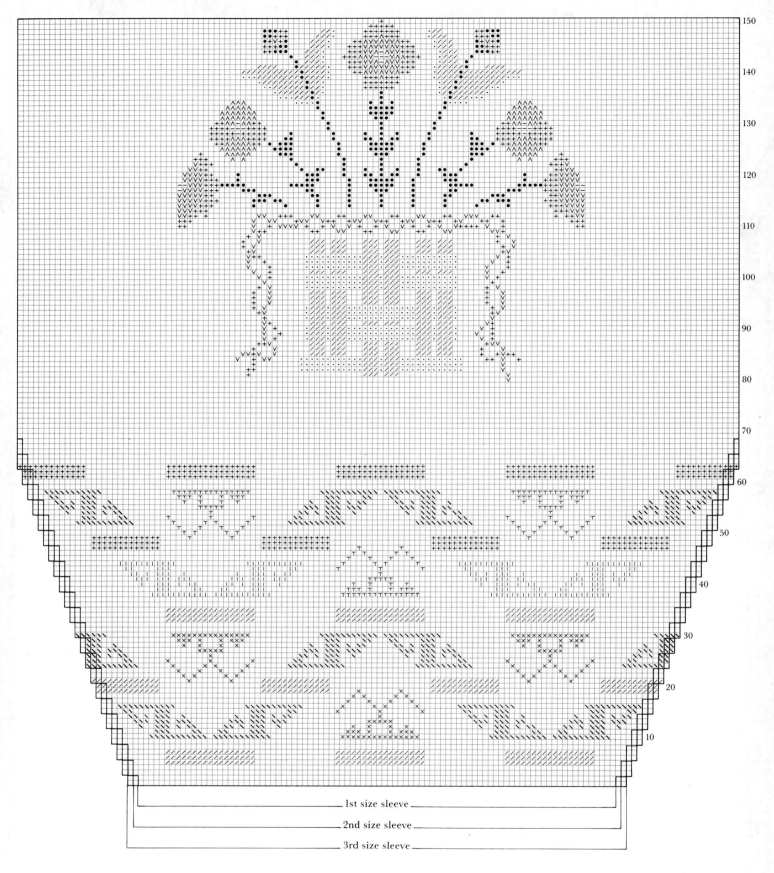

1st size sleeve

2nd size sleeve

3rd size sleeve

A B C D E F G H J L M N Q

A back view of the Sicily cardigan.

Make buttonholes
1st buttonhole row Rib 17[19,21], cast off 2 sts, * rib 25 including st used to cast off, cast off 2 sts; rep from * to last 4 sts, rib to end.
2nd buttonhole row Rib to end, casting on 2 sts over those cast off in previous row.
Rib 4 rows more.
Cast off in rib.

NECKBAND
Join both shoulder seams.
With rs of work facing, using 2¼mm (US1) needles and yarn A, K up 37[39,41] sts across top of buttonhole band and up right front neck edge, K 53[55,57] from spare needle at back neck, inc 1 st at centre, and K up 37[39,41] sts down left front neck edge and across button band. 128[134,140] sts.
Work 4 rows in K1, P1 rib.
Make buttonhole
1st buttonhole row Rib 122[128,134], cast off 2 sts, rib to end.
2nd buttonhole row Rib to end casting 2 sts over those cast off in previous row.
Rib 4 rows.
Cast off loosely in rib.

TO MAKE UP
Set in sleeves, easing to fit around cast-off sts at underarm.
Join side and sleeve seams.
Sew on buttons.

NOSEGAY

This pattern was inspired by an Ottoman embroidery. The flowers sprout from a 'horn of plenty', the ancient symbol of agricultural prosperity and wealth, or general good, easy living under a sunny sky! I like the delicacy of the flowers in this design, the Islamic 'moon and star' motif that repeats on the back of the waistcoat – and the design's overall light, summery feel.

SIZES
To fit: 91[96,101]cm (36[38,40]in) bust
Actual width measurement: 94[99,104]cm (37[39,41]in)
Back length: 46[57·5,48·5]cm (18[18¾, 19¼]in)
Front length: 54[55·5,56·5]cm (21¼[22, 22¼]in)

MATERIALS
225[250,250]g (8[9,9]oz) four-ply cotton in white (A)
50g (2oz) in pastel blue (B)
25g (1oz) each in royal blue (C), sky (D), wine (E), purple-grey (F), canary (G), pale blue-green (H), salmon (J), mulberry (L), bright rose (M), mauve pink (N), mid-blue (Q) and pale mauve (R)
1 pair each 2¼mm (US1) and 2¾mm (US2) needles
4 buttons

TENSION
34 sts and 43 rows to 10cm (4in) over patt on 2¾mm (US2) needles.
Note: Work colour patt by the intarsia method, see page 141.

BACK
Using 2¼mm (US1) needles and yarn A, cast on 145[153,161] sts. Work 7 rows in K1, P1 rib.
Next row Rib 3[7,4], * make 1, rib 10[10,11]; rep from * ending last rep rib 2[6,3]. 160[168, 176] sts.

CHART 1

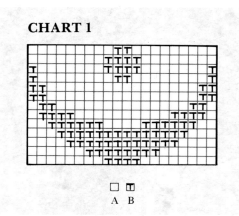

□ ⊤
A B

Change to 2¾mm (US2) needles and beg colour patt from chart 1 working in st st throughout as foll:
1st row (rs) K to end in A.
2nd row P to end in A.
3rd row K10[14,18]A, * patt 1st row of chart 1, 40A; rep from * once more, patt 1st row of chart 1, 10[14,18]A.
This row sets position of chart 1 motif.
4th-15th rows Cont as set until chart 1 motifs are completed.
16th-22nd rows Work in st st in A, beg with a P row.
23rd row K40[44,48]A, patt 1st row of chart 1, 40A, patt 1st row of chart 1, 40[44,48]A.
This row sets position of chart 1 motifs.
24th-35th rows Cont as set until chart 1 motifs are completed.
36th-54th rows Work in st st in A, beg with a P row.
55th row K5[9,13]A, * patt 1st row of chart 1, 45A; rep from * once more, patt 1st row of chart 1, 5[9,13]A.
This row sets position of chart 1 motifs.
56th-67th rows Cont as set until chart 1 motifs are completed.
68th-74th rows Work in st st in A, beg with a P row.
75th row K35[39,43]A, patt 1st row of chart 1, 50A, patt 1st row of chart 1, 35[39,43]A.
This row sets position of chart 1 motifs.
76th-87th rows Cont as set until chart 1 motifs are completed.
88th-106th rows Work in st st in A, beg and ending with a P row.
1st size only
Shape armholes
107th row Cast off 4 sts, K66A including st used to cast off, patt 1st row of chart 1, K70A. 156 sts.
This row sets position of chart 1 motif.
108th-119th rows Cont as set until chart 1 is completed, *at the same time* cast off 4 sts at beg of next row and dec 1 st at each end of foll 9 rows, then dec 1 st at each end of next alt row. 132 sts.
120th-126th rows Work in st st in yarn A, *at the same time* cont to dec as set on foll 3 alt rows. 126 sts.

A really wonderful photograph that shows how these garments can be dressed up to look glamorous enough for evening wear.

NOSEGAY CHART 2

210
200
190
180
170
160
150
140
130
120
110
100
90
80
70
60
50
40
30
20
10

3rd size left front
2nd size left front
1st size left front

1st size left front
2nd size left front
3rd size left front

☐ A
⊓ B
☒ C
⊡ D
⊟ E
◩ F
⊔ G
◪ H
◩ J
⊙ L
◩ M
⊞ N
◪ Q
◫ R

127th row K2 tog with A, K11A, patt 1st row of chart 1, 60A, patt 1st row of chart 1, 11A, K2 tog with A. 124 sts.
This row sets position of chart 1 motifs.
128th-139th rows Cont as set until chart 1 motifs are completed, *at the same time* cont to dec on alt rows until 116 sts rem.
2nd and 3rd sizes only
107th row K74[78]A, patt 1st row of chart 1, K 74[78]A.
This row sets position of chart 1.
108th-110th[112th] rows Cont as set, work 3[5] more rows of chart 1 motif.
Shape armholes
111th[113th] row Cast off 4 sts, patt to end.
112th[114th] row Cast off 4 sts patt to end.
113th[115th]-126th rows Cont in chart motif as set, then work 7 rows in st st in A, *at the same time* dec 1 st at each end of every foll 11[12] rows, then on foll alt row for 2nd size only, ending with a ws row. 136[144] sts.
127th row K2 tog with A, K16[20]A, patt 1st row of chart 1, K60A, patt 1st row of chart 1, K to last 2 sts in A, K2 tog. 134[142] sts.
This row sets position of chart 1.
Cont as set until chart 1 motifs are completed, then work in st st in A only, *at the same time* dec on every alt row as set until 120[124] sts rem.

All sizes
Now work straight in st st in A until 158 rows have been worked from top of rib, ending with a ws row.
159th row K48[50,52]A, patt 1st row of chart 1, K48[50,52]A.
This row sets position of chart 1.
Cont as set until chart 1 is completed.
Now work in st st in A until 178 rows have been worked from top of rib.
179th row K3[5,7]A, patt 1st row of chart 1, K70A, patt 1st row of chart 1, K3[5,7]A.
This row sets position of chart 1 motifs.
Cont as set until chart 1 is completed.
Work 1[7,11] rows in st st in A, ending with a ws row.
Shape shoulders
Cast off 12[13,13] sts at beg of next 4 rows, then 13[12,13] sts at beg of foll 2 rows. 42[44,46] sts.
Change to 2¼mm (US1) needles and work 8 rows in K1, P1 rib.
Cast off loosely in rib.

LEFT FRONT
Using 2¾mm (US2) needles and yarn A, cast on 2 sts.

Work in st st in A, beg with a K row, cast on 2 sts at beg of next row, 3 sts at beg of foll row, 2 sts at beg of next row and 2[2,3] sts at beg of foll row. 11[11,12] sts.
** Now cast on 3 sts at beg of next row and 2 sts at beg of foll row. **
Rep from ** to ** 3 times more. 31[31,32] sts.
Now cast on 3[3,4] sts at beg of next row, 2 sts at beg of foll row, 3[4,4] sts at beg of next row, 2 sts at beg of next row and 3[4,4] sts at beg of foll row. 44[46,48] sts.
Now cast on 1[2,2] sts at beg of next row, 4 sts at beg of foll row, 1[1,2] sts at beg of next row and 4 sts at beg of foll row. 54[57,60] sts.
Inc 1 st at beg of next row, cast on 4[4,5] sts at beg of foll row, inc 1 st at beg of next row, then cast on 4[5,5] sts at beg of foll row (25 rows have been worked from cast-on row.) 64[68,72] sts.
Now beg colour patt from chart 2, beg with 26th chart row, working in st st throughout as foll:
26th row (ws) Inc 1 P-wise in first st, P18[19,21]A, 1C, 44[47,49]A.
This row sets position of chart 2 patt.
Cont as set, *at the same time* cast on 5 sts at beg of next row, inc 1 st at beg of foll row, cast on 6 sts at beg of next row and inc 1 st at beg of foll row. 78[82,86] sts.
Now work straight until 127[131,133] rows have been worked from cast-on edge, ending with a rs row.
Shape neck
Keeping patt correct, dec 1 st on next and 2 foll 4th rows ending with a ws row. 75[79,83] sts.
Shape armhole
Keeping patt correct, cast off 4 sts at beg of next row. 71[75,79] sts.
Now dec 1 st at armhole edge on next 9[11,13] rows, then foll 9 alt rows, *at the same time* cont to dec at neck edge on every 4th row as before until 19[20,21] decs in all have been made at neck edge (200[208,214] rows have been worked from cast-on row). 37[38, 39] sts.
Now work straight until 222[228,232] rows have been worked from cast-on row (when chart 2 is completed, cont in A only), ending at armhole edge.
Shape shoulder
Cast off 12[13,13] sts at beg of next and foll alt row. 13[12,13] sts.
Work 1 row.
Cast off.

RIGHT FRONT

Work as given for left front, reversing all shapings and chart 2 patt.

BUTTON BAND

With rs of work facing, using 2¼mm (US1) needles and yarn A, K up 85[87,89] sts from shoulder to beg of front neck shaping, K up 80[83,84] sts to end of front point shaping, K up 36[37,38] sts to cast-on edge, K up 1 st from cast-on edge, and mark it, and K up 58[60,62] sts to side edge. 260[268,274] sts. Work in K1, P1 rib as foll:
1st row (ws) (P1, K1) to end.
2nd row P1, (K1,P1) to marked st, make 1, K marked st, make 1, rib to end. 262[270,276] sts.
Keeping rib correct, work 6 more rows, inc on alt rows as before.
Cast off loosely in rib.

BUTTONHOLE BAND

With rs of work facing, using 2¼mm (US1) needles and yarn A, K up 58[60,62] sts from side edge to cast-on edge, K up 1 st from cast-on edge and mark it, K up 36[37,38] sts to end of front point shaping, K up 80[83,84] sts to beg of front neck shaping, and K up 85[87,89] sts to shoulder. 260[268,274] sts.
1st row (ws) (K1, P1) to end.
2nd row (K1, P1) to marked st, make 1, K1, make 1, rib to end.
Work 6 more rows in K1, P1 rib as set, *at the same time* make buttonholes on foll 2nd and 3rd rows as foll:
1st buttonhole row Rib to marked st, make 1, K marked st, make 1, rib 37[38,39], cast off 2 sts, * rib 24[25,25] including st used to cast off, cast off 2 sts; rep from * twice more, rib to end.
2nd buttonhole row Rib to end, casting on 2 sts over those cast off in previous row.
Complete as for button band.

TO MAKE UP

Join shoulder seams.
Armbands
With rs of work facing, using 2¼mm (US1) needles and yarn A, K up 166[172,178] sts evenly around armhole edge.
Work 7 rows in K1, P1 rib.
Cast off loosely in rib.
Join side and armband seams.
Sew on buttons.

This is a variation of the Nosegay design made up as a sweater – here in a black colourway.

A neatly styled, short cardigan, this is simpler to knit than most of our designs, using far fewer colours and thicker yarn. Most of the contrast colours are in cotton chenille, giving a lovely textured look to the classically composed design.

SIZES
To fit: 91[96]cm (36[38]in) bust
Actual width measurement: 88·5[92·5]cm (35[36½]in)
Length: 44[45]cm (17½[17¾]in)
Sleeve seam: 50cm (19¾in)

MATERIALS
400[450]g (15[16]oz) Aran-weight wool in buttermilk (A)
100g (4oz) each in periwinkle (B), cloud blue (C), french mustard (D) and old rose (E)
50g (2oz) each in lavender (F) and old gold (G)
1 pair each 3¼mm (US4) and 4½mm (US7) needles
6 buttons

TENSION
21 sts and 28 rows to 10cm (4in) over patt on 4½mm (US7) needles.
Note: Work colour patt by the intarsia method, see page 141.

BACK
Using 3¼mm (US4) needles and yarn A, cast on 85[89] sts.
Work in K1, P1 rib as foll:
1st row (rs) (K1, P1) to last st, K1.
2nd row (P1, K1) to last st, P1.
Rep these 2 rows 3 times more, then 1st row again. **
Next row Rib 2[4], * make 1, rib 10; rep from * ending last rep rib 3[5]. 94[98] sts.
Change to 4½mm (US7) needles and beg colour patt from chart 1, working in st st throughout between back markers, work 44[48] rows.
Shape armholes
Keeping patt correct, cast off 4 sts at beg of next 2 rows. 86[90] sts.
Now work straight until chart 1 is completed. Work 2 rows st st in A.
Shape shoulders
Cast off 14 sts at beg of next 2 rows, then 13[14] sts at beg of foll 2 rows.
Leave rem 32[34] sts on a spare needle.

LEFT FRONT
Using 3¼mm (US4) needles and yarn A, cast on 39[41] sts.
Work as given for back to **.
Next row Rib 2, * make 1, rib 9; rep from * ending last rep rib 1[3]. 44[46] sts.
Change to 4½mm (US7) needles and beg colour patt from chart 1, working between left front markers, work 44[48] rows, ending with a ws row.
Shape armhole
Keeping chart patt correct, cast off 4 sts at beg of next row. 40[42] sts.
Now work straight until 101[103] rows have been worked from top of rib, ending at neck edge.
Shape neck
Keeping patt correct, cast off 3 sts at beg of next row, then dec 1 st at neck edge on foll 10[11] rows (when chart 1 is completed cont in A only). 27[28] sts.
Work 6[7] rows straight ending at armhole edge (118[122] rows have been worked from top of rib).
Shape shoulder
Cast off 14 sts at beg of next row. 13[14] sts.
Work 1 row.
Cast off.

RIGHT FRONT
Work as given for left front, working between right front markers on chart 1, and reversing shapings.

SLEEVES
Using 3¼mm (US4) needles and yarn A, cast on 43 sts.
Work 9 rows in K1, P1 rib as given for back cardigan.
Next row Rib 2, * make 1, rib 4; rep from * ending last rep rib 1. 54 sts.
Change to 4½mm (US7) needles and work 30 rows in st st, *at the same time* inc 1 st at each end of every foll 4th row. 68 sts.
Now beg colour patt from chart 2 as foll:
Next row K22A, 1D, 21A, 1D, 23A.
This row sets position of chart 2.
Keeping incs correct, cont as set until there are 102 sts (when chart 2 is completed, cont in A only).
Now work straight until sleeve measures 50cm (19¾in) from cast-on edge, ending with a ws row. Cast off.

(Previous page) A composed, serene shot taken in the frescoed bedroom of a Tuscan villa. In the soft light the blues and creams of the sweater harmonize with the faded colours of the room.

WOODROSE CHART 1   Omit motifs 1 and 2 completely from the fronts.

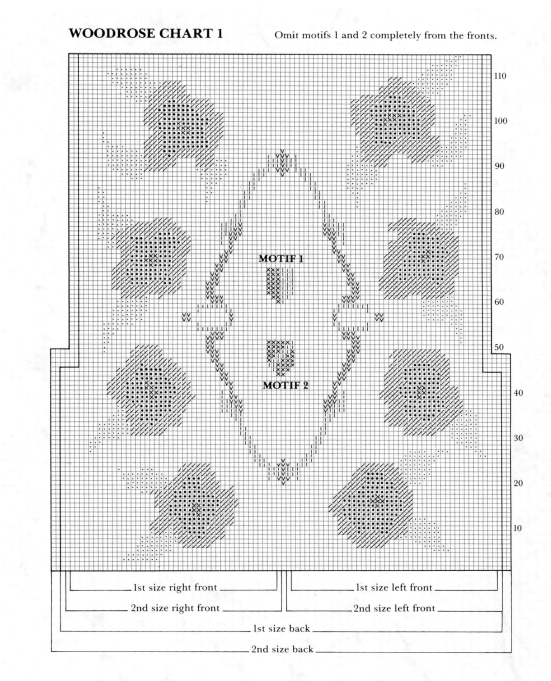

A
B
C
D
E
F
G

MOTIF 1

MOTIF 2

1st size right front
2nd size right front
1st size left front
2nd size left front
1st size back
2nd size back

BUTTON BAND
With rs of work facing, using 3¼mm (US4) needles and yarn A, K up 82[84] sts down left front edge from beg of neck shaping to cast-on edge.
Work 6 rows in K1, P1 rib.
Cast off in rib.

BUTTONHOLE BAND
With rs of work facing, using 3¼mm (US4) needles and yarn A, K up 82[84] sts up right front edge from cast-on edge to beg of neck shaping.
Work 2 rows in K1, P1 rib as given for back of cardigan.

Make buttonholes
1st buttonhole row Rib 12[14], cast off 2 sts; * rib 14 including st used to cast off, cast off 2 sts; rep from * 3 times more, rib to end.
2nd buttonhole row Rib to end casting on 2 sts over those cast off in previous row.
Rib 2 rows.
Cast off in rib.

TO MAKE UP
Join shoulder seams.
Neckband
With rs of work facing using 3¼mm (US4) needles and yarn A, K up 5 sts across top of buttonhole band, 20[22] sts up right front

WOODROSE CHART 2

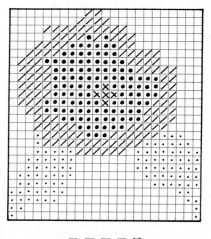

A B C D G

neck, K across 32[34] sts left on spare needle at back neck, K up 20[22] sts down left front neck and 5 sts across top of button band. 82[88] sts.

Work 2 rows in K1, P1 rib.

Make buttonhole

1st buttonhole row Rib 78[84] sts, cast off 2 sts, rib to end.

2nd buttonhole row Rib to end, casting on 2 sts over those cast off in previous row.

Rib 2 rows.

Cast off loosely in rib.

Set in sleeves, easing to fit around cast-off sts at underarm.

Join side and sleeve seams.

Sew on buttons.

The back of the Woodrose cardigan.

This design is another of my own great favourites. I took a basic layout – diamond shapes on a lattice grid – that could be very flat and dull, then brought it to life with bright colours, textured knitting in the form of bobbles, grapes and strawberries, and exuberant motifs that burst out of their diamond confines. It all results in one of our liveliest, most summery designs, complemented by the full, slightly cropped, squarish style with its wide slash neck. The script is a quote from a poem by Catullus, a Roman poet writing in the first century BC: 'Let us live and love'.

SIZES
To fit: 91[96,101]cm (36[38,40]in) bust/chest
Actual width measurement: 104[109,114]cm (41[43,45]in)
Length: 57[58·5,59·5]cm (22½[23,23½]in)
Sleeve seam: 46[47,48]cm (18¼[18½,19]in)

MATERIALS
400[400,425]g (15[15,16]oz) four-ply cotton in black (A)
50g (2oz) each in pastel blue (B) and cornflower (C)
25g (1oz) each in pastel green (D), dove grey (E), purple (F), canary (G), lavender (H), blue-green (J), light blue (L), blue (M), mid-green (N), mulberry (Q), pale turquoise (R), pale beige (S), washed straw (T), mid-grey (U), mauve-pink (V), cherry (W), natural (X), terracotta (Y) and nut brown (Z)
1 pair each 2¼mm (US1) and 2¾mm (US2) needles

TENSION
33 sts and 41 rows to 10cm (4in) over chart patt on 2¾mm (US2) needles.
Note: Work colour patt by the intarsia method, see page 143.

SPECIAL INSTRUCTIONS
Strawberry motif
1st row (rs) Patt to strawberry symbol, with W, (K1, P1, K1) into next st, patt to end.
2nd row Patt to strawberry symbol, with W, (P1, K1) into next st, P1, (K1, P1) into next st, patt to end.
3rd row Patt to strawberry symbol, with W, K1, (P1, K1) into next st, (K1, P1, K1) into next st, (K1, P1) into next st, K1, patt to end of row.
4th row Patt to strawberry symbol, P2W, 1B, 3W, 1B, 2W, turn, K9W, turn, P1W, 1B, 2W, 1B, 2W, 1B, 1W, patt to end.
5th row Patt to strawberry symbol, K9W, patt to end.
6th row Patt to strawberry symbol, P2W, 1B, 2W, 1B, 3W, turn, K9W, turn, P9W, patt to end.

7th row Patt to strawberry symbol, * pass 2nd, 3rd and 4th sts on left-hand needle over 1st st and K this st in W,* K1N, rep from * to * again, patt to end.
8th row Patt to within 1 st of strawberry symbol, pass 2nd st on left-hand needle over 1st st and P this st in B, P1N, P2 tog in B, patt to end.
These 8 rows form strawberry motif.

Reverse stocking stitch
P right-side rows and K wrong-side rows.

Make bobble
Using colour shown in bobble symbol, (K1, P1, K1, P1, K1) into next st, turn, P5, turn, K5, turn, P5, turn, K5, turn, P5, turn, pass 2nd, 3rd, 4th and 5th sts over 1st st and off needle, K this st.

BACK AND FRONT (alike)
Using 2¼mm (US1) needles and yarn A, cast on 167[175,183] sts.
Work in twisted rib as foll:
1st row (rs) K1 tbl, * P1, K1 tbl; rep from * to end of row.
2nd row P1, * K1 tbl, P1; rep from * to end of row.
Rep these 2 rows 8 times more, then 1st row again.
Next row Rib 4[8,12], * make 1, rib 40; rep from * ending last rep rib 3[7,11]. 172[180, 188] sts.
Change to 2¾mm (US2) needles and beg colour patt as foll:
1st-8th rows Work in st st in A, beg with a K row.
9th-10th rows K to end in C.
11th row P to end in C.
12th row K to end in C.
13th row K to end in A.
14th row P to end in A.
15th-22nd rows Work in patt from chart 1, working in st st throughout, beg with K row.
23rd row K to end in A.
24th row P to end in A.
25th-26th rows K to end in J.

The photograph on the previous page shows the black colourway of the Diamonds sweater (given in the pattern), the one opposite; the cream colourway. The first was shot by some bathing huts on the Italian coast, the second in an orchard in the Tuscan hills – two contrasting moods, but both equally evocative of warm, summer days.

DIAMONDS CHART 2

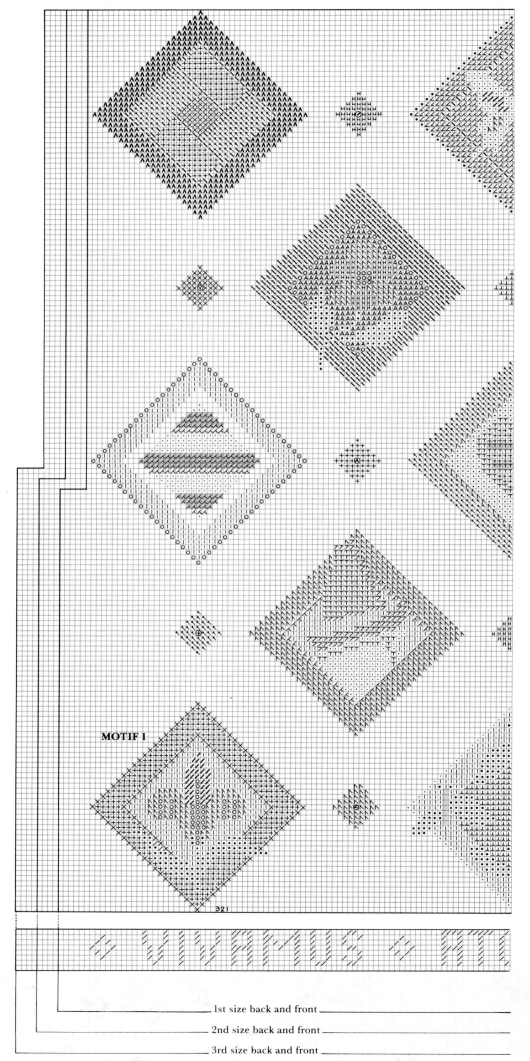

□ A
⊞ B
⊡ C
◪ D
◩ E
◧ F
☒ G
⊞ H
◩ J
◪ L
◪ M
⊡ N
◪ Q
◪ R
◪ S
⊤ T
⊥ U
⊞ V
☒ W
◪ X
◯ Y
◪ Z

◯ make
   bobble
   in colour
   shown.

▨ make
   strawberry
   in T over
   8 rows as
   shown on
   page 32.

Work all
other tinted
areas in
rev st st
in colour
indicated by
the symbol.

MOTIF 1

DIAMONDS CHART 1

1st size back and front _____

2nd size back and front _____

3rd size back and front _____

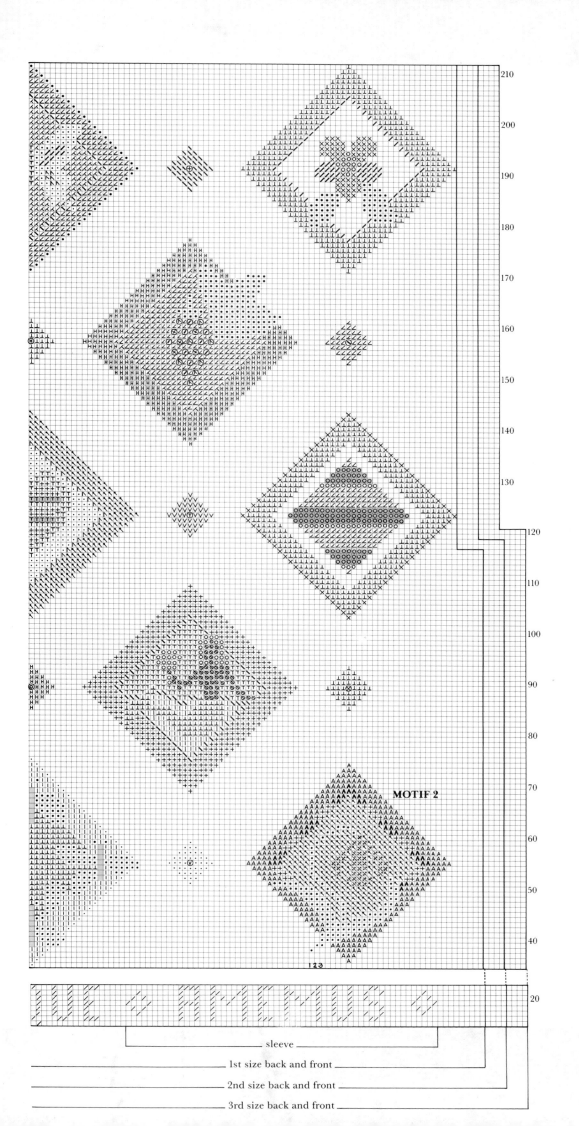

Note: work in st st unless
otherwise indicated.

MOTIF 2

Omit motifs 1 and 2
completely from the sleeves.

1 1st size sleeve markers.

2 2nd size sleeve markers.

3 3rd size sleeve markers.

210
200
190
180
170
160
150
140
130
120
110
100
90
80
70
60
50
40
20

123

sleeve

1st size back and front

2nd size back and front

3rd size back and front

27th row P to end in J.
28th row K to end in J.
29th row K to end in A.
30th-34th rows Work in st st in A, beg with a P row.
Now work in colour patt from chart 2, working in st st unless otherwise indicated on chart, beg with a K row, until 116[118,120] rows have been completed from top of rib, ending with a ws row.
Shape armholes
Cast off 5 sts at beg of next 2 rows. 162[170,178] sts.
Now work 96[100,102] rows straight (when chart 2 patt is complete, cont in A only), ending with a ws row.
Shape shoulders
Next row Sl 13[14,15] sts on to a stitch holder, patt to end.
Rep last row 3 times more.
Now sl 14[15,16] sts on to a stitch holder at beg of next 2 rows. 82[84,86] sts.
Cast off very neatly.

SLEEVES
Using 2¼mm (US1) needles and yarn A, cast on 67[69,71] sts.
Work 39 rows in twisted rib as given for back.
Next row Rib 6[6,8], * make 1, rib 4; rep from * ending last rep rib 5[7,7]. 82[84,86] sts.
Change to 2¾mm (US2) needles and work in colour patt as foll:
1st-14th rows Work as given for 1st-14th rows of back, *at the same time* inc 1 st at each end of 3rd, 6th, 9th and 12th rows. 90[92,94] sts.
Now work in patt from chart 1, working between sleeve markers as foll:
15th row With A, inc 1 in 1st st, K to last st, inc 1. 92[94,96] sts.
16th row P27[28,29]A, 1X, 2A, 1X, 2A, 1X, 5A, 1X, 2A, 3X, 2A, 1X, 5A, 1X, 3A, 2X, 4A, 2X, P to end in A.
17th row K18 [19,20]A, 1X, 7A, 1X, 2A, 1X, 2A, 1X, 2A, 1X, 2A, 1X, 5A, 1X, 4A, 1X, 2A, 1X, 5A, 1X, 2A, 1X, 2A, 1X, 7A, 1X, K to end in A.
The last 2 rows set position of chart 1.
Cont as set, work 18th-22nd chart rows, inc on next and foll 3rd row as before. 96[98,100] sts.
23rd-32nd rows Work as given for 23rd-32nd rows of back, inc as before on 24th, 27th and 30th rows. 102[104,106] sts.

33rd row K to end in Q, inc 1 st at beg and end of row. 104[106,108] sts.
34th row K to end in Q.
35th row P to end in Q.
36th row K to end in Q, inc 1 st at beg and end of row. 106[108,110] sts.
37th-40th rows Work in st st in A, beg with a K row and inc 1 st at beg and end of 39th row. 108[110,112] sts.
Now beg colour patt from chart 2, working between sleeve markers and in st st unless otherwise indicated on chart, *at the same time* cont to inc 1 st at each end of 3rd rows as before until there are 168[174,178] sts (129[135,138] rows have been worked from top of rib).
Now work 23[21,22] rows straight, complete whole motifs, then work in A only.
Cast off.

TO MAKE UP
Finish shoulders
With rs of work facing using 2¾mm (US2) needles and yarn A, sl sts left on stitch holder at left back shoulder on to left-hand needle. 40[43,46] sts.
K 1 row.
Leave these sts on a spare needle.
Rep for left front, right back and right front shoulders.
Graft shoulders
Place left front shoulder and left back shoulder together with wrong sides facing. Using 2¾mm (US2) needles and yarn A, K tog 1st st of one front shoulder with 1st st of back. Cont in this way across the row.
Cast off neatly on right side.
Rep for right front and right back shoulder. Set in sleeves, easing to fit around cast-off sts at underarm.
Join side and sleeve seams.

(Left)
The detail shows the sailing boat motif from the cream Diamonds sweater.

(Right)
The navy blue version photographed in the late afternoon light of a Tuscan hilltop village in September.

(Overleaf)
The cream and black colourways of Diamonds with (left) a variation for men. It has slightly different motifs and a traditional fisherman's jersey shape.

The main picture shows Circles (page 67) with (from top left, anticlockwise) Paisley (page 47), Fars (page 61), Boteh (page 42), and the Susani T-shirt (page 52) in the bluebell colourway.

BOTEH

'Boteh' is another word for the paisley motif which has spread worldwide from its ancient Eastern origins. The bold 'botehs' in this design are typical of Afshari tribal rugs from Persia – though I have recoloured them in a random, jazzy way to turn a sober traditional design into a modern fashionable one.

SIZES
To fit: one size only up to 106cm (42in) bust/chest
Actual width measurement: 124·5cm (49in)
Length: 66·5cm (26¼in)
Sleeve seam: 55cm (21¾in)

MATERIALS
450g (16oz) double knitting wool in dark blue (A)
75g (3oz) each in iris (B), red (C), brown (D), mid blue (E), pale fawn (F) and ruby (G)
50g (2oz) each in khaki (H), gold (J), dark green (L) and black (M)
1 pair each 3mm (US3) and 3¾mm (US5) needles

TENSION
26 sts and 29 rows to 10cm (4in) over patt on 3¾mm (US5) needles.
Note: Work colour patt by the intarsia method, see page 141.

BACK
Using 3mm (US3) needles and yarn A, cast on 145 sts.
Work in twisted rib as foll:
1st row (rs) K1 tbl, * P1, K1 tbl; rep from * to end of row.
2nd row P1, * K1 tbl, P1; rep from * to end of row.
Rep these 2 rows 15 times more then 1st row again.
Next row Rib 8, * make 1, rib 8; rep from * ending last rep rib 9. 162 sts.
Change to 3¾mm (US5) needles and beg colour patt from chart 1, working in st st throughout, work 86 rows, end with a ws row.
Shape armholes
Cast off 4 sts at beg of next 2 rows.
154 sts. **
Work 76 rows straight (when chart patt is completed, cont in A only), end with a ws row.
Shape shoulders
Cast off 18 sts at beg of next 4 rows, then 17 sts at beg of foll 2 rows.
Leave rem 48 sts on a spare needle until required for neckband.

FRONT
Work as given for back to **.
Work 55 rows straight, ending with a rs row.
Divide for neck
Next row Patt 70 sts and leave these sts on a spare needle, patt 14 sts and leave these sts on a stitch holder for neckband, then patt to end. 70 sts.
Cont on these sts only for left side of neck.
Work 1 row.
Cast off 3 sts at beg of next and foll 2 alt rows, then dec 1 st at neck edge on next 8 rows (when chart patt is completed, cont in A only). 53 sts.
Work 8 rows straight, ending with a ws row.
Shape shoulder
Cast off 18 sts at beg of next and foll alt row.
17 sts. Work 1 row. Cast off.
With rs of work facing, return to 70 sts on spare needle, rejoin yarn to inner edge, patt to end.
Complete right side of neck to match left side, reversing shapings.

SLEEVES
Using 3mm (US3) needles and yarn A, cast on 63 sts.
Work 33 rows in twisted rib as for back.
Next row Rib 2, * make 1, rib 3; rep from * ending last rep rib 1. 84 sts.
Change to 3¾mm (US5) needles and beg colour patt working from chart 2, *at the same time* inc 1 st at each end of every 4th row until there are 148 sts (when chart 2 is completed, cont in A only).
Work 2 rows straight. Cast off.

TO MAKE UP
Join right shoulder seam.
Neckband
With rs of work facing, using 3mm (US3) needles and yarn A, K up 24 sts down left front neck, K14 from stitch holder at centre front, K up 24 sts up right front neck, K48 from spare needle at back neck. 110 sts.
Work 10 rows in K1, P1 rib.
Cast off loosely in rib.
Join left shoulder and neckband seam.
Set in sleeves, easing to fit around cast-off sts at underarm. Join side and sleeve seams.

An evening shot by the river Arno which flows through Florence to the sea below Pisa. This was taken beside the Roman bridge at Lucca.

BOTEH CHART 1

A unless
otherwise
indicated

⊞ A
◪ B
◩ C
◪ D
◪ E
◪ F
◪ G
⊡ H
⊟ J
⊞ L
⊡ M

BOTEH CHART 2

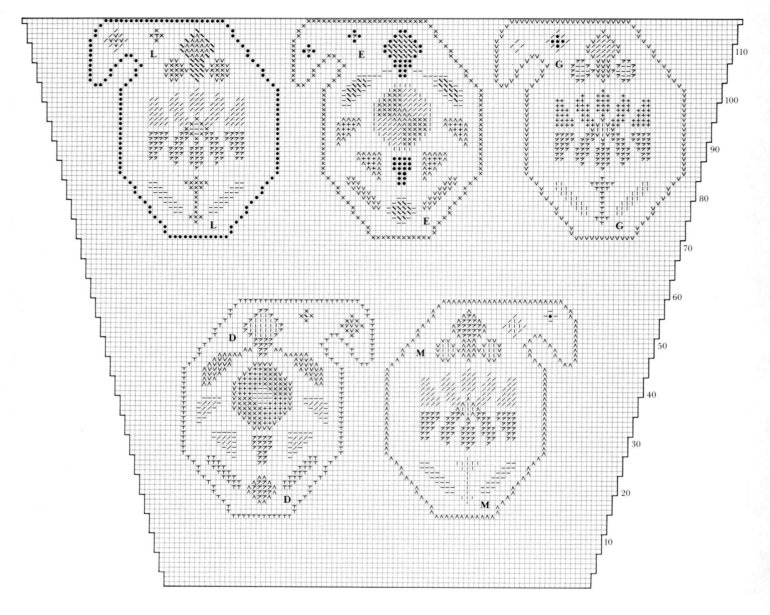

A unless
otherwise
indicated

A B C D E F G H J L M

PAISLEY CHART

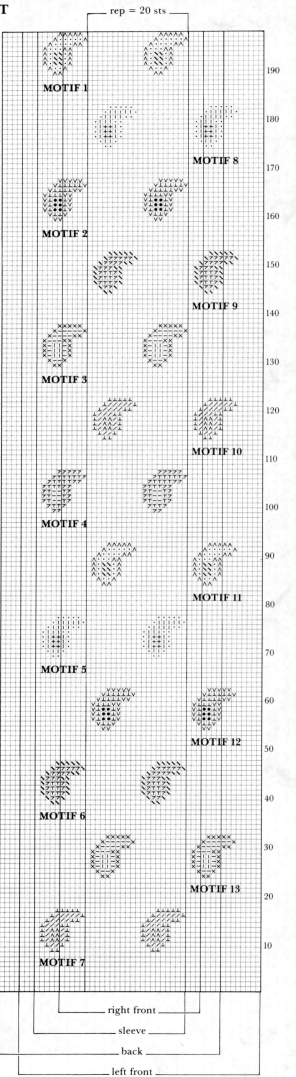

rep = 20 sts

MOTIF 1

MOTIF 8

190

180

170

160

MOTIF 2

MOTIF 9

150

140

MOTIF 3

130

Omit motifs
1 to 7
completely
from the
left-hand
edge of the
right front.

Omit motifs
8 to 13
completely
from the
right-hand
edge of the
right front
or back.

MOTIF 10

120

110

MOTIF 4

100

90

MOTIF 11

80

MOTIF 5

70

60

MOTIF 12

50

MOTIF 6

40

30

MOTIF 13

20

MOTIF 7

10

right front

sleeve

back

left front

☐ A
⊞ B
☑ C
◹ D
⊠ E
⊟ F
⊡ G
◺ H
◪ J
⊞ L
☑ M
⊡ N
⊡ Q
⊞ R

*(Previous page)
The marble
walls of a 14th-
century church
provide a cool
backdrop for
the zingy
fuchsia of the
cardigan.*

Though the style of this garment and the colourway are brand new, the actual paisley pattern is the earliest of my designs to appear in this book. Despite this, it remains firmly in my top ten. The pattern is subtle and understated, almost classic, but it is a great vehicle for multifarious new colour combinations. Over the years we have produced it in cotton, wool, alpaca and silk as a sweater, a waistcoat and a cardigan. This shawl-collared cardigan, designed especially for the book, is the latest and, I think, the most successful of its manifestations.

SIZE
To fit: one size only up to 101cm (40in) bust
Actual width measurement: 111cm (43¾in)
Length: 57cm (22½in)
Sleeve seam: 46·5cm (18¼in)

MATERIALS
425g (16oz) four-ply wool in fuchsia (A)
25g (1oz) each in slate blue (B), light blue (C), lilac fleck (D), flecked grey-blue (E), dark chilli (F), lavender (G), streaked slate blue (H), gentian (J), mid blue-green (L), warm purple (M), peacock (N), old rose (Q) and grey-green fleck (R)
1 pair each 2¼mm (US1) and 2¾mm (US2) needles
6 buttons

TENSION
33 sts and 39 rows to 10cm (4in) over patt on 2¾mm (US2) needles.
Note: Work colour patt by the intarsia method, see page 141.

BACK
Using 2¼mm (US1) needles and yarn A, cast on 163 sts.
Work in twisted rib as foll:
1st row (rs) K1 tbl, * P1, K1 tbl; rep from * to end of row.
2nd row P1, * K1 tbl, P1; rep from * to end of row.
Rep these 2 rows 16 times more, then 1st row again.
Next row Rib 2, * make 1, rib 8; rep from * ending last rep rib 1. 184 sts.
Change to 2¾mm (US2) needles and beg colour patt from chart, working in st st throughout between back markers, as foll:
1st-8th rows Work in st st in A.
9th row K7A, * 5A, 2B, 13A; rep from * to last 17 sts, 5A, 2B, 10A.
10th row P9A, 1B, 2C, 1B, 4A, * 12A, 1B, 2C, 1B, 4A; rep from * to last 7 sts, 7A.
These 2 rows set position of chart patt. Cont as set until 104 rows have been worked from top of rib, ending with a ws row.

Shape armholes
Keeping patt correct, cast off 5 sts at beg of next 2 rows. 174 sts.
Now work straight until chart is completed (197 rows have been completed from top of rib).

Shape shoulders
Cont in st st in A, cast off 19 sts at beg of next 6 rows. 60 sts.
Cast off.

LEFT FRONT
Using 2¼mm (US1) needles and yarn A, cast on 87 sts.
Work in K1, P1 rib for front band and twisted rib as foll:
1st row K1 tbl, * P1, K1 tbl; rep from * to last 10 sts, (P1, K1) 5 times.
2nd row (P1, K1) 5 times, P1, * K1 tbl, P1; rep from * to end of row.
Rep these 2 rows 16 times more, then 1st row again.
Next row (P1, K1) 5 times, (P1, K1 tbl) twice, * make 1, (P1, K1 tbl) 3 times, P1, make 1, (K1 tbl, P1) 3 times, K1 tbl; rep from * ending last rep P1, K1 tbl, P1. 98 sts.
Change to 2¾mm (US2) needles and beg colour patt from chart, keeping 10 sts in K1, P1 rib correct throughout as foll:
1st row (rs) K88A, (K1, P1) to end in A.
2nd row (P1, K1) 5 times in A, P to end in A.
3rd-8th rows Rep 1st-2nd rows 3 times more.
9th row K15A, * 5A, 2B, 13A; rep from * 4 times ending last rep K6A, (P1, K1) 5 times in A.
10th row (P1, K1) 5 times in A, P5A, 1B, 2C, 1B, 4A, * 12A, 1B, 2C, 1B, 4A; rep from * to last 15 sts, P15A.
The last 10 rows set position of chart patt and K1, P1 rib.
Cont as set until 104 rows have been worked from top of rib, ending with a ws row.

Shape armhole
Cast off 5 sts at beg of next row. 93 sts.
Now work straight until 121 rows have been worked from top of rib, ending with a rs row.

Next row Rib 10 sts, then sl these sts on to a stitch holder for front band, patt to end. 83 sts. Work 1 row.

Shape neck

Keeping patt correct, dec 1 st at neck edge on next and every foll 3rd row until 57 sts rem (when chart patt is completed cont in A only).

Now work straight until 206 rows in all have been worked from top of rib, ending at armhole edge.

Shape shoulder

Cast off 19 sts at beg of next and foll alt row. 19 sts.

Work 1 row.

Cast off.

RIGHT FRONT

Work as given for left front, reversing position of front band and all shapings, and working st st part between right front markers, *at the same time* make buttonholes on 3rd-4th rows of front band as foll (instructions refer to 10 sts in K1, P1 rib worked for front band only):

Make buttonhole

1st buttonhole row Rib 4, cast off 3 sts, rib 3 including st used to cast off.

2nd buttonhole row Rib 10, casting on 3 sts over those cast off in previous row.

Rep 1st-2nd buttonhole rows on 35th-36th rib rows, then on foll 27th-28th rows.

Work 28 rows, then rep 1st-2nd buttonhole rows again.

Now rep last 30 rows until 6 buttonholes in all have been worked (the 6th buttonhole will have been worked on 117th-118th rows from top of rib).

I particularly like the collar of Paisley for the way it lies on the shoulders, suggesting the easy lines of a shawl.

SLEEVES

Using 2¼mm (US1) needles and yarn A, cast on 71 sts.

Work 35 rows in twisted rib as given for back.

Next row Rib 8, * make 1, rib 3; rep from * ending last rep rib 9. 90 sts.

Change to 2¾mm (US2) needles and yarn A and beg colour patt from chart, working in st st throughout, between sleeve markers, *at the same time* inc 1 st at each end of every foll 4th row until there are 170 sts, working the incs into patt (160 rows have been worked from top of rib).

Work 2 rows in st st in A. Cast off.

LEFT FRONT COLLAR

Using 2¾mm (US2) needles and yarn A, with rs of work facing, rejoin yarn to inner edge of sts left on stitch holder at neck edge. 10 sts.

Cont in K1, P1 rib as set, *at the same time* inc 1 st at right-hand (inner) edge of every row, working the incs *in rev st st* (ws of collar) in A, until there are 25 sts, thus ending with a P row.

Now beg colour patt from chart as foll:

16th row Rib 10A, K8A, 2J, 4A, inc in next st in A. 26 sts.

17th row Inc 1 in A, P4A, 1J, 2L, 1J, 7A, rib to end in A.

These 2 rows set position of one motif on 99th and 100th rows of chart patt.

Cont as set reading odd-numbered rows as P rows and even-numbered rows as K rows, *at the same time* keeping incs correct, until there are 66 sts, working the incs into patt.

Now work straight until 105 rows have been worked in st st, ending with a 188th patt row.

Work 1 row in A. Cast off, leaving 10 sts in rib on a stitch holder.

RIGHT FRONT COLLAR

Work as given for left front collar, reversing shaping and beg colour patt on 16th row as foll:

16th row Rib 10A, P5A, 2J, 7A, inc in next st in A. 26 sts.

17th row Inc 1 in A, K7A, 1J, 2L, 1J, 4A, rib to end in A. 27 sts.

These 2 rows set position of one motif on 99th-100th rows of chart patt.

Cont as set reading odd-numbered rows on chart as P rows and even-numbered rows on chart as K rows.

Complete as given for left front collar.

BACK COLLAR

Using 2¾mm (US2) needles and yarn A, cast on 20 sts. K 1 row.

Work in st st, beg with a P row, *at the same time* cast on 5 sts at beg of next 6 rows, then 4 sts at beg of foll 3 rows. 62 sts.

Next row Cast on 4 sts, K12A, (2M, 18A), twice, 2M, 12A.

Next row Cast on 4 sts, P15A, (1M, 2B, 1M, 16A) twice, 1M, 2B, 1M, 11A.

These 2 rows set position of 3 motifs on 54th-55th rows of chart patt.

Cont in chart patt as set *at the same time* cast on 4 sts at beg of next 3 rows. 82 sts.

Work 1 row.

Now dec 1 st each end next 9 rows. 64 sts.

Cont to dec as set, work 5 rows in st st in A. 54 sts.

Next row K2A tog, K14A, 2Q, 18A, 2Q, 14A, K2Atog. 52 sts.

This row sets position of 2 motifs on 69th row of chart patt.

Keeping decs and patt correct, cont as set, work 15 rows.

Keeping decs correct, cont in st st in A only until 2 sts rem, K2A tog.

Fasten off.

TO MAKE UP

Join shoulder seams.

With rs of collar and ws of front tog, join shaped edges of front collars to front neck edges, so that rs of collar folds on to rs of front.

With rs of collar and ws of back tog, join straight part of collar to back neck on each side, left and right collar sections meeting neatly at centre back.

Join row-end edges of back collar to cast-off sections of left and right front collar so that cast-off edge of back collar finishes neatly at centre back.

Back collar band

Using 2¾mm (US2) needles and yarn A, rib across 10 sts left on stitch holder at left front collar.

Work in K1, P1 rib until band fits around outer edge of back collar to right front collar, joining band to collar edge as work progresses.

Graft 10 sts of back collar band to 10 sts left on stitch holder at right front collar.

Set in sleeves, easing to fit around cast-off sts at underarm.

Join side and sleeve seams.

Sew on buttons.

SUSANI

This v-neck, short cardigan goes very well with the T-shirt as a twin-set, though either one works quite happily on its own. 'Susani' is a type of near-Eastern needlework that tends towards bold flower motifs in bright colours. For the navy and the cream colourways, however, I have used rather soft colours; for the bluebell T-shirt (see page 41) I went to town with nice hot yellows and tangerines – completely changing the design's character.

SIZES
To fit: 91[96,102]cm (36[38,40]in) bust
Cardigan
Actual width measurement: 103[108,113]cm (40½[42½,44½]in)
Length: 50[51,53]cm (19¾[20,21]in)
Sleeve seam: 44[45,46]cm (17¼[17¾,18]in)
T-shirt
Actual width measurement: 101[106,111]cm (39¾[41¾,43¾]in)
Length: 48[49,50]cm (19[19¼,19¾in)
Sleeve seam: 18·5[19,19·5]cm (7¼[7½,7¾]in)

MATERIALS
Cardigan
350[400,400]g (13[15,15]oz) four-ply cotton in navy (A)
50g (2oz) each in salmon (B), mulberry (C), natural (D)
25g (1oz) each in pastel pink (E), washed straw (F), pale beige (G), pale grey (H), deep blue (J) and pale bleached green (L)
T-shirt
300[350,375]g (11[13,14]oz) four-ply cotton in ecru (A)
50g (2oz) each in salmon (B), mulberry (C) and soft mid blue (D)
25g (1oz) each in pastel pink (E), washed straw (F), pale beige (G), pale grey (H), deep blue (J) and pale bleached green (L)
1 pair each 2¼mm (US1) and 2¾mm (US2) needles
5 buttons (cardigan only)

TENSION
32 sts and 41 rows to 10cm (4in) over patt on 2¾mm (US2) needles.
Note: Work colour patt by the intarsia method, see page 141.

CARDIGAN BACK
Using 2¼mm (US1) needles and yarn A, cast on 147[155,163] sts.
Work in twisted rib as foll:
1st row (rs) K1 tbl, * P1, K1 tbl; rep from * to end of row.
2nd row P1, * K1 tbl, P1; rep from * to end of row.

Rep these 2 rows 8 times more, then 1st row again.
Next row Rib 2[6,10], * make 1, rib 9; rep from * ending last rep rib 1[5,9]. 164[172,180] sts.
Change to 2¾mm (US2) needles and beg colour patt from chart 1, working in st st throughout, as foll:
1st row (rs) K17[21,25]A, patt 1st row of chart 1, K to end in A.
2nd row P16[20,24]A, patt 2nd row of chart 1, P to end in A.
These 2 rows set position of chart 1.
Cont as set until 76[78,82] rows have been completed, ending with a ws row.
Shape armholes
Cast off 5 sts at beg of next 2 rows. 154[162,170] sts.
Now work straight until 190[194,200] rows have been worked from top of rib, ending with a ws row (when chart 1 is completed, cont in A only).
Shape shoulders
Cast off 16[17,18] sts at beg of next 6 rows. 58[60,62] sts. Cast off.

CARDIGAN LEFT FRONT
Using 2¼mm (US1) needles and yarn A, cast on 71[75,79] sts.
Work 19 rows in twisted rib as given for back.
Next row Rib 4[6,8], * make 1, rib 8; rep from * ending last rep rib 3[5,7]. 80[84,88] sts. **
Change to 2¾mm (US2) needles and work in colour patt from chart 1 between left front markers as foll:
1st-4th rows Work in st st in A.
5th row K44[46,48]A, 2B, 34[36,38]A.
6th row P33[35,37]A, 4B, 43[45,47]A.
These 6 rows set position of chart patt.
Cont as set until 61 rows have been worked from top of rib, ending with a rs row.
Now work in patt from chart 2 as foll:
62nd row P54[56,58]A, 1H, 25[27,29]A.
63rd row K24[26,28]A, 3H, 53[55,57]A.
These 2 rows set position of chart 2.
Cont as set until 76[78,82] rows have been

The navy blue Susani cardigan, worn here as a twinset with the navy version of the T-shirt. This is worked in all the same colours as the cardigan.

180
170
160
150
140
130
120
110
100
90
80
70
60
50
40
30
20
10

G   G   H   H

L   L   G   G

cardigan right front _____   _____ cardigan left front _____

_____ cardigan back and T-shirt back and front _____

worked from top of rib, ending with a ws row.

Shape armhole

Cast off 5 sts at beg of next row. 75[79,83] sts.

Now work straight until 105 rows have been worked from top of rib (when chart 2 is completed cont in A only), ending with a rs row.

Now work in patt from chart 1, working between left front markers and beg with 106th row as foll:

106th row P38[40,42]A, 2D, 35[37,39]A.

107th row K34[36,38]A, 4D, 37[39,42]A.

These 2 rows set position of chart 1. ***

Cont as set until 131[133,137] rows have been worked from top of rib, ending with a rs row.

Shape neck

Keeping chart 1 patt correct, dec 1 st at neck edge on next and every foll alt row until 48[51,54] sts rem (when chart 1 is completed cont in A only).

Now work straight until 192[196,202] rows have been worked from top of rib, ending at armhole edge.

Shape shoulder

Cast off 16[17,18] sts at beg of next and foll alt row. 16[17,18] sts.

Work 1 row.

Cast off.

CARDIGAN RIGHT FRONT

Work as given for left front to **.

Change to 2¾mm (US2) needles and work in patt from chart 1 between right front markers as foll:

1st-4th rows Work in st st in A.

5th row K34[36,38]A, 2E, 44[46,48]A.

6th row P43[45,47]A, 4E, 33[35,37]A.

These 2 rows set position of chart 1.

Cont as set until 63 rows have been worked from top of rib, ending with a rs row.

Now work in patt from chart 3 as foll:

64th row P23[25,27]A, 2H, 55[57,59]A.

65th row K51[53,55]A, 2E, 2A, 2H, 5A, 2E, 16[18,20]A.

These 2 rows set position of chart 3.

Cont as set, work 11[13,17] rows, ending with a rs row.

Shape armhole

Cast off 5 sts at beg of next row. 75[79,83] sts.

Now work straight until chart 3 is completed (101 rows in all have been worked from top of rib).

Work 4 rows in st st in A.

Now work in patt from chart 1 between right front markers beg with 106th row as foll:

106th row P35[37,39]A, 2B, 38[40,42]A.

107th row K37[39,41]A, 4B, 34[36,38]A.

These 2 rows set position of chart 1.

Complete as given for left front, from *** to end, reversing shapings.

CARDIGAN SLEEVES

Using 2¼mm (US1) needles and yarn A, cast on 69[71,73] sts.

Work 23 rows in twisted rib as for back.

Next row Rib 4[6,6], * make 1, rib 3; rep from * ending last rep rib 5[5,7]. 90[92,94] sts.

Change to 2¾mm (US2) needles and beg colour patt from chart 4, *at the same time* inc 1

A unless otherwise indicated

☑ B
☐ C
◉ D
☒ E
◣ F
⊞ G
☑ H
◩ J
◫ L

SUSANI CHART 2

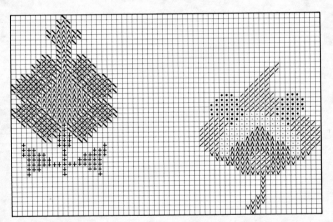

SUSANI CHART 3

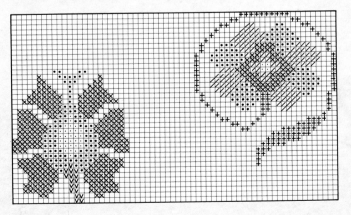

140

130

120

110

100

90

80

70

60

50

40

30

20

10

G   G   H   H

L   L

1st size cardigan sleeve
2nd size cardigan sleeve
3rd size cardigan sleeve

SUSANI CHART 5

T-shirt sleeve motif

T-shirt back and front

☐	A unless otherwise indicated
☑	B
⊡	C
⊡	D
⊠	E
◩	F
⊞	G
☑	H
◪	J
⊡	L

st at each end of every 3rd row until there are 194[198,202] sts (when chart 4 is completed, cont in A only).
Work straight until 164[168,172] rows have been worked from top of rib.
Cast off.

CARDIGAN FRONT BAND
Using 2¼mm (US1) needles and yarn A, cast on 10 sts.
Work 4 rows in K1, P1 rib.
**** Make buttonhole
1st buttonhole row Rib 4, cast off 2 sts, rib to end.
2nd buttonhole row Rib to end, casting on 2 sts over those cast off in previous row.
Work 26[26,28] rows in K1, P1 rib.
Rep from **** 3 times more.
Rep 1st and 2nd buttonhole rows again.
Cont in rib until 454[464,472] rows have been worked from cast-on edge (or until

band when slightly stretched fits up right front, around back neck and down left front).
Cast off in rib.

TO MAKE UP CARDIGAN
Join shoulder seams.
Set in sleeves, easing to fit around cast-off sts at underarm.
Join side and sleeve seams.
Join on front band, matching fifth button-hole to beg of front neck shaping and stretching slightly to fit around front opening edges and across back neck.
Sew on buttons.

T-SHIRT BACK
Using 2¼mm (US1) needles and yarn A, cast on 162[170,178] sts. Work 14 rows in twisted rib as for cardigan back.
Change to 2¾mm (US2) needles and beg colour patt from chart 1 as foll:

1st-4th rows Work in st st in A.
5th row K44[48,52]A, 2B, 70A, 2E, 44[48,52]A.
6th row P43[47,51]A, 4E, 68A, 4B, 43[47,51]A.
These 2 rows set position of chart 1.
Cont as set until 105 rows have been worked from chart 1, ending with a rs row.
Now beg colour patt from chart 5 as foll:
106th row P47[51,55]A, 2B, 64A, 2D, 47[51,55]A.
107th row K46[50,54]A, 4D, 62A, 4B, 46[50,54]A.
These 2 rows set, position of chart 5.
Cont as set work 1[3,7] rows, ending with a ws row.
Shape armholes
Cast off 4 sts at beg of next 2 rows. 154[162,170] sts.
Now keeping patt correct, dec 1 st at each end of next and every alt row until 122[126,130] sts rem (141[147,155] rows have been worked from top of rib). *****
Now work 43[41,39] rows straight, ending with a ws row (when chart 5 is completed cont in A only).
Shape shoulders
Cast off 11[12,12] sts at beg of next 4 rows, then 12[11,12] sts at beg of foll 2 rows. 54[56,58] sts.
Cast off.

T-SHIRT FRONT
Work as given for back to *****.
Now work straight as for back until 159[161,165] rows have been worked from top of rib, ending with a rs row.
Divide for neck
Next row Patt 55[56,57] sts and leave these sts on a spare needle, cast off 12[14,16] sts, patt to end. 55[56,57] sts.
Cont on these sts only for left side of neck. Work 1 row.
Cast off 3 sts at beg of next and foll 4 alt rows.
Now dec 1 st at neck edge until 34[35,36] sts rem.
Work 10[12,14] rows straight, ending at armhole edge.
Shape shoulder
Cast off 11[12,12] sts at beg of next and foll alt row. 12[11,12] sts.
Work 1 row. Cast off.
With rs of work facing return to sts on spare needle, rejoin yarn to next st, patt to end of row. 55[56,57] sts.

Complete right side of neck to match left side reversing shaping.

T-SHIRT SLEEVES
Using 2¼mm (US1) needles and yarn A, cast on 98[100,102] sts.
Work 10 rows in twisted rib as given for cardigan back.
Change to 2¾mm (US2) needles and work 10 rows in st st, *at the same time* inc 1 st at each end of every 4th row. 102[104,106] sts.
Now beg colour patt from chart 5, working between sleeve markers as foll:
Next row K50[51,52]A, 2B, 50[51,52]A.
This row sets position of chart 5 sleeve motif.
Cont as set, *at the same time* inc on next and every foll 4th row as before until there are 130[134,136] sts (when 52 rows of chart 5 have been completed, cont in A only).
Now work straight until 68[70,72] rows have been completed, ending with a ws row.
Shape top
Cast off 4 sts at beg of next 2 rows, then 3 sts at beg of foll 20 rows, and 8 sts at beg of next 6 rows. 14[18,20] sts.
Cast off.

COLLAR
Using 2¼mm (US1) needles and yarn A, cast on 138[144,150] sts.
Work in K1, P1 rib until collar measures 9cm (3½in).
Cast off in rib.

TO MAKE UP
Join shoulder seams.
Join on cast-on edge of collar to neck edge so that row-end edges meet neatly at centre front.
Set in sleeves.
Join side and sleeve seams.

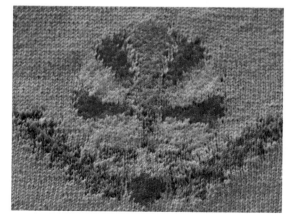

Worn slightly oversize, the Susani T-shirt, here in cream, gives a very nice, easy look. The detail shows the bluebell version, illustrating how different the design looks in hot colours.

*A back view
of the Susani
cardigan in
navy.*

Fars is a province in Southern Persia where the most wonderful carpets and rugs are woven by the nomadic tribes. As well as the more usual geometric and formal patterns, Farsi rugs contain lively, idiosyncratic representations of men, women, chickens, dogs, flowers, trees and bushes – anything, in fact, that might catch the weaver's eye. This design, which is just as good on men or women, features a gang of fairly ferocious-looking tribesmen dressed in the South Persian equivalent of their Sunday-best.

SIZES

To fit: 91[96,101]cm (36[38,40]in) bust/chest
Actual width measurement: 96[101,106]cm
(38[40,41¾]in)
Length: 60[61·5,62·5]cm (23½[24¼,24½]in)
Sleeve seam: 44·5[45·5,46·5]cm (17½[18, 18¼]in)

MATERIALS

400[400,425]g (15[15,16]oz) four-ply wool in cream (A)
50g (2oz) each in grey-brown (B), red (C), mid blue (D), gold (E), fawn (F), gentian (G), light olive (H)
25g (1oz) each in bottle green (J), black (L), dark rust (M), lilac fleck (N), sky blue (Q) and pale blue (R)
1 pair each 2¼mm (US1) and 2¾mm (US2) needles
2¼mm (US1) circular needle
2 buttons

TENSION

34 sts and 41 rows to 10cm (4in) over patt on 2¾mm (US2) needles.
Note: Work colour patt by the intarsia method, see page 141.

FRONT

Using 2¼mm (US1) needles and yarn A, cast on 143[151,159] sts.
Work in twisted rib as foll:
1st row (rs) K1 tbl, * P1, K1 tbl; rep from * to end of row.
2nd row P1, * K1 tbl, P1; rep from * to end of row.
Rep these 2 rows 20 times more, then 1st row again.

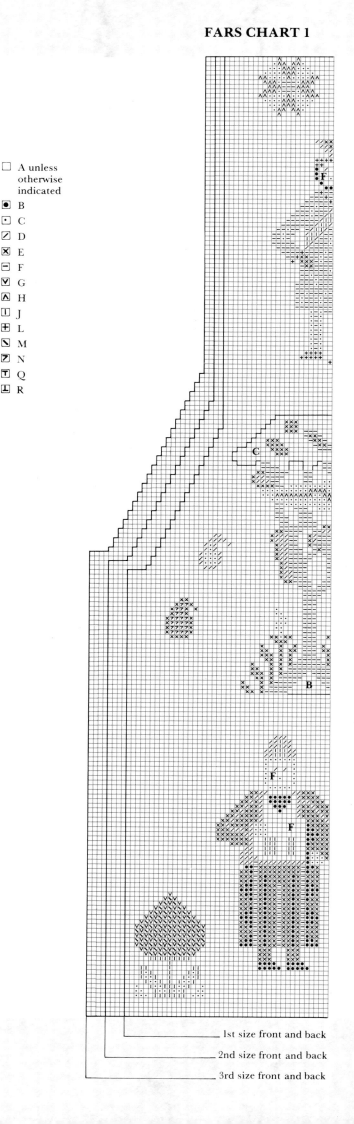

☐ A unless otherwise indicated
⊡ B
⊡ C
☑ D
☒ E
⊟ F
☑ G
⊼ H
⊡ J
⊞ L
☒ M
☑ N
⊤ Q
⊥ R

1st size front and back
2nd size front and back
3rd size front and back

3rd
2nd

1st
size

F

F

F

F

F

C

B

L

H

D

200

190

180

170

160

150

140

130

120

110

100

90

80

70

60

50

40

30

20

10

1st size front and back

2nd size front and back

3rd size front and back

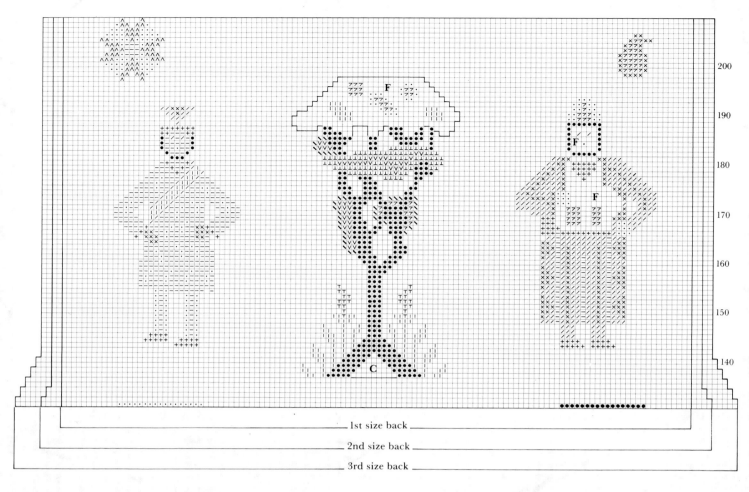

Next row Rib 2[6,10], * make 1, rib 7; rep
from * ending last rep rib 1[5,9]. 164[172,180]
sts.
Change to 2¾mm (US2) needles and beg
colour patt from chart 1, working in st st
throughout, work 96[98,100] rows, ending
with a ws row.

Shape armholes
Keeping patt correct, cast off 4 sts at beg of
next 2 rows, then dec 1 st at each end of next
and foll 15[17,19] alt rows. 124[128,132] sts.
Now work straight until 151[155,157] rows
have been worked from chart, ending with a
rs row.

Divide for front opening
Next row Patt 58[60,62] sts and leave these
sts on a spare needle for right side of neck,
patt 8 sts and leave on a stitch holder for
front band, patt to end. 58[60,62] sts.
Cont on these sts only for left side of neck.
Work straight until 187[191,193] rows in all
have been worked from chart, ending at
inner edge.

Shape neck
Cast off 4 sts at beg of next row, then 3 sts at
beg of foll 4 alt rows. Now dec 1 st at neck

edge on next 7[8,9] rows. 35[36,37] sts.
Now work straight until 214[220,224] rows
have been worked from chart, ending at
armhole edge.

Shape shoulder
Cast off 12 sts at beg of next and foll alt row.
11[12,13] sts.
Work 1 row.
Cast off.
With rs of work facing, return to sts left on
spare needle, rejoin yarn to inner edge, patt
to end. 58[60,62] sts.
Complete right side of neck to match left
side, reversing shapings.

BACK
Work 130 rows from chart 1 as given for
front.
Now keeping armhole shaping correct, cont
in patt from chart 2 so that 131st patt row is
1st row of chart 2, work 10 rows. 124[128,132]
sts.
Now keeping chart 2 patt correct, work
72[78,82] rows straight (when chart 2 is
completed cont in A only), ending with a
ws row.

☐	A unless otherwise indicated
⊡	B
⊡	C
☑	D
☒	E
⊟	F
☑	G
◪	H
⊡	J
⊞	L
◩	M
◪	N
⊤	Q
⊥	R

Shape shoulders

Cast off 12 sts at beg of next 4 rows, then 11[12,13] sts at beg of foll 2 rows.

Leave rem 54[56,58] sts on a spare needle.

SLEEVES

Using 2¼mm (US1) needles and yarn A, cast on 67[69,71] sts.

Work 43 rows in twisted rib as given for back.

Next row Rib 4[4,6], * make 1, rib 2; rep from * ending last rep rib 3[5,5]. 98[100,102] sts.

Change to 2¾mm (US2) needles and beg colour patt from chart 3, working in st st throughout, *at the same time* inc 1 st at each end of every 3rd row until there are 194[200,204] sts (when chart 3 is complete, cont in A only).

Work 4[2,3] rows straight.

Shape top

Cast off 4 sts at beg of next 2 rows, then 3 sts at beg of foll 16[18,18] rows, and 10 sts at beg of next 8 rows. 58[58,62] sts.

Work 1 row.

Cast off.

BUTTONHOLE BAND

With rs of work facing, using 2¼mm (US1) needles and yarn A, K10 from stitch holder at centre front as foll:

1st row K3, make 1, K2, make 1, K3. 10 sts.

Work in K1, P1 rib as foll:

Next row (K1, P1) to end.

Rep this row 14 times more.

Make buttonhole

1st buttonhole row Rib 3, cast off 4 sts, rib 3.

2nd buttonhole row Rib to end casting on 4 sts over those cast off in previous row.

Rib 14 rows.

Rep 1st–2nd buttonhole rows.

Rib 4 rows.

Cast off 5 sts, leave rem 5 sts on a stitch holder for collar.

BUTTON BAND

Using 2¼mm (US1) needles and yarn A, cast on 10 sts.

Work 38 rows in K1, P1 rib as given for buttonhole band.

Cast off 5 sts, leave rem 5 sts on a stitch holder for collar.

TO MAKE UP

Join shoulder seams.

Sew left-hand row-end edge of buttonhole band to right front opening.

Sew cast-on edge of button band inside K-up edge of buttonhole band, with 5 sts left on stitch holder adjacent to neck edge. Sew right-hand row-end edge to left front opening.

Collar

With rs of work facing, using 2¼mm (US1) circular needle and yarn A, work in K1, P1 rib across 5 sts left on stitch holder at top of buttonhole band, K up 37[39,41] sts up right front neck edge, K across 54[56,58] sts left on spare needle at back neck, K up 37[39,41] sts down left front neck, then work in rib across 5 sts left on stitch holder at top of button band. 138[144,150] sts.

Work in K1, P1 rib until collar measures 10cm (4in).

Cast off loosely in rib.

Set in sleeves. Join side and sleeve seams.

Sew on buttons.

The close-up, showing the black version of Fars, illustrates well how varying the colour of the detailing in each motif gives the design movement and life.

FARS CHART 3

A unless otherwise indicated   B C D E F G H J L M N Q R

CIRCLES

CIRCLES CHART

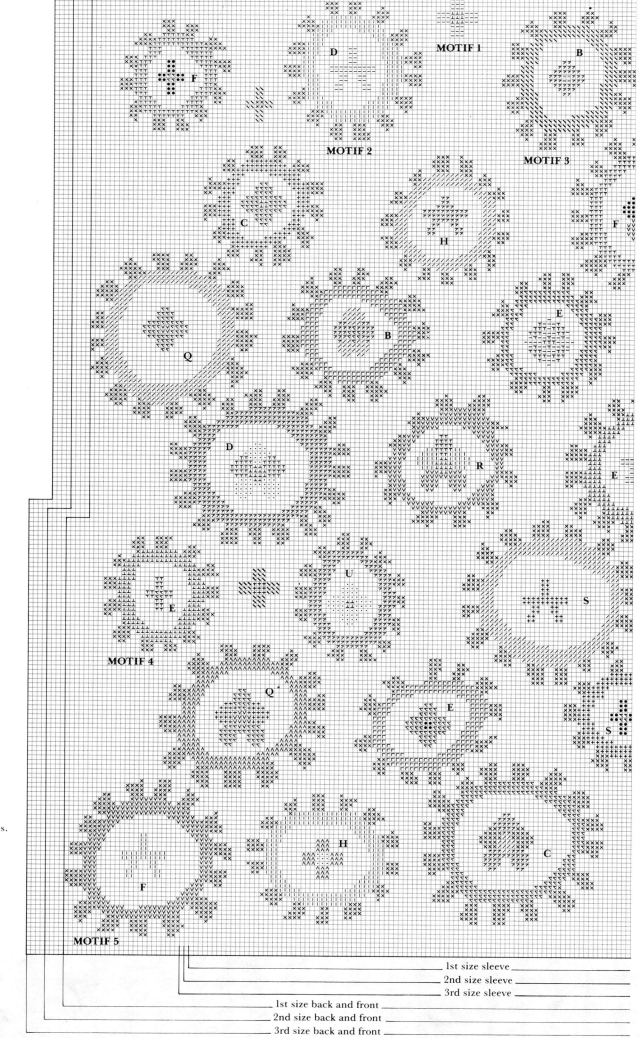

A unless
otherwise
indicated

☒ B
☑ C
☒ D
◉ E
⊥ F
Ⅱ G
◰ H
◺ J
⊡ L
◩ M
◪ N
▭ Q
⊞ R
◿ S
⊤ T
⊟ U

Work motifs
4 and 5 on
the back
and front only.
Omit
completely
from the sleeves.

MOTIF 1
MOTIF 2
MOTIF 3
MOTIF 4
MOTIF 5

1st size sleeve
2nd size sleeve
3rd size sleeve
1st size back and front
2nd size back and front
3rd size back and front

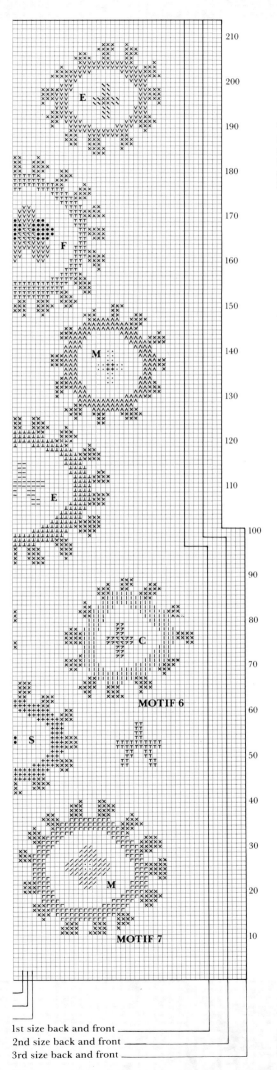

210

200

190 Work motifs
1, 2 and 3 on
the back only.
180 Omit
completely
from the front.

170

160

150

140

130

120

110

100

90

80

70

MOTIF 6 60

50

Work motifs
6 and 7 on
the back
40 and front only.
Omit
completely
from the sleeves.
30

20

MOTIF 7 10

Note: sleeve
begins on
3rd chart row.

1st size back and front
2nd size back and front
3rd size back and front

I saw this pattern on a woven cap worn by a woman sitting opposite me on a London Underground train. I think it is probably an Afghani or maybe a Nepali pattern. I had to study the hat pretty carefully to memorize the pattern, at the same time hoping that the woman wouldn't get off at the next stop – and taking care not to stare too obviously and risk her getting entirely the wrong impression! The sweater looks good on both men and women. The 'cogs' around each circle give the pattern a liveliness and movement that it might otherwise lack; while the circles themselves allow great opportunities for playing around with colour.

SIZES
To fit: 91[96,101]cm (36[38,40]in) bust/chest
Actual width measurement: 106[111,116]cm (41¾[43¾,45¾]in)
Length: 65[66,67]cm (25½[26,26½]in)
Sleeve seam: 48·5[50,51]cm (19[19¾,20]in)

MATERIALS
425[450,450]g (15[16,16]oz) four-ply cotton in black (A)
100g (4oz) in pale beige (B)
50g (2oz) each in blue (C), maroon (D) and dark grey (E)
25g (1oz) each in gold (F), airforce blue (G), mid-grey (H), fresh green (J), peacock (L), mauve pink (M), clear blue-green (N), pale mauve (Q), terracotta (R), sky (S), mid-blue (T) and lavender (U)
1 pair each 2¼mm (US1) and 2¾mm (US2) needles

TENSION
31 sts and 39 rows to 10cm (4in) over patt on 2¾mm (US2) needles.
Note: Work colour patt by the intarsia method, see page 141.

BACK
Using 2¼mm (US1) needles and yarn A, cast on 143[151,159] sts. Work in twisted rib as foll:
1st row (rs) K1 tbl, * P1, K1 tbl; rep from * to end of row.
2nd row P1, * K1 tbl, P1; rep from * to end.

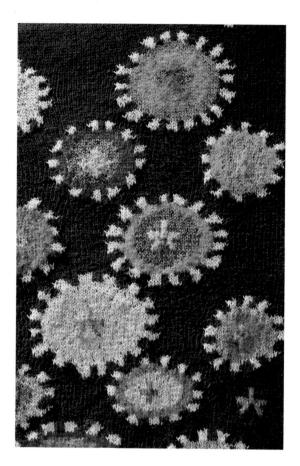

Rep these 2 rows 20 times more, then 1st row again.
Next row Rib 2[6,10], * make 1, rib 7; rep from * ending last rep rib 1[5,9]. 164[172,180] sts.
Change to 2¾mm (US2) needles and beg colour patt from chart, working in st st throughout, work 96[98,100] rows, ending with a ws row.
Shape armholes
Cast off 5 sts at beg of next 2 rows. 154[162,170] sts. **
Now work 114[118,120] rows straight (when chart is completed cont in A only), ending with a ws row.
Shape shoulders
Cast off 17[18,19] sts at beg of next 4 rows, then cast off 16[17,18] sts at beg of foll 2 rows.
Leave rem 54[56,58] sts on a spare needle.

FRONT
Work as given for back to **.
Now work 89[91,91] rows straight, ending with a rs row.
Divide for neck
Next row Patt 71[74,77] sts and leave these

sts on a spare needle, patt 12[14,16] sts and leave these sts on a stitch holder, patt to end. 71[74,77] sts.
Cont on these sts only for left side of neck. Work 1 row.
Cast off 3 sts at beg of next and foll 4 alt rows, then dec 1 st at neck edge on foll 6 rows. 50[53,56] sts.
Now work straight until front matches back to beg of shoulder shaping, ending at armhole edge. Work 2 rows.
Shape shoulder
Cast off 17[18,19] sts at beg of next and foll alt row. 16[17,18] sts.
Work 1 row. Cast off.
With rs of work facing return to sts on spare needle, rejoin yarn to inside edge, patt to end.
Work 1 row.
Complete right side of neck to match left side, reversing shapings.

SLEEVES
Using 2¼mm (US1) needles and yarn A, cast on 67[69,71] sts.
Work 43 rows in twisted rib as for back.
Next row Rib 4[4,6], * make 1, rib 2; rep from *, ending last rep rib 3[5,5]. 98[100,102] sts.
Change to 2¾mm (US2) needles and beg colour patt from chart, working between sleeve markers, *at the same time* inc 1 st at each end of every 3rd row until there are 196[202,206] sts; work only whole circle motifs, then cont in A only. (147[153,156] rows of chart have been completed.)
Work 3[3,4] rows straight.
Cast off.

TO MAKE UP
Join right shoulder seam.
Neckband
With rs of work facing, using 2¼mm (US1) needles and yarn A, K up 33[34,35] sts down left front edge, K across 12[14,16] sts from stitch holder at centre front, K up 33[34,35] sts up right front neck, and K across 54[56,58] sts from spare needle at centre back. 132[138,144] sts.
Work 6·5cm (2½in) in K1, P1 rib.
Cast off loosely in rib.
Join left shoulder and neckband seam.
Set in sleeves, matching centre of cast-off edge to shoulder seam and easing to fit around cast-off sts at underarm.
Join side and sleeve seams.

One of the advantages of abstract patterns is that you are not tied in any way to a particular colour scheme — you can colour just as you like. I've done Circles design on black, cream, white, dark purple and light blue backgrounds, and could happily go on to do several more. The detail on this page shows the colours of some of the circles in close-up.

GARDENS & MEADOWS

The main picture shows Fruits (page 80) with (from top left, anticlockwise) the dark brown version of Basia in wool and silk (page 74), Garden cardigan in cream (page 85), Roses & Ribbons in Iris (page 91) and Tartan (page 96).

BASIA

I like this design very much. The idea for it came from Elizabethan samplers, which I admire for their delicate stitchwork, but especially because they are often so personal, being worked as love-tokens or as exhortations to good behaviour. The writing here is from a poem by Catullus: '*Da mi basia mille, deinde centum,/Dein mille altera, dein secunda centum,/Deinde usque altera mille, deinde centum,*' which translates: 'Give me a thousand kisses, then a hundred, then another thousand, then a second hundred, then yet another thousand, then a hundred'.

It's a good Valentine's Day sweater!

SIZES
To fit: 91[96,101]cm (36[38,40]in) bust
Actual width measurement: 106[111,116]cm (41¾[43¾,45¾]in)
Length: 64[65,66]cm (25¼[25½,26]in)
Sleeve seam: 49[51,52]cm (19¼[20,20½]in)

MATERIALS
400[400,450]g (15[15,16]oz) four-ply cotton in blue (A)
50g (2oz) each in pale green (B) and pale grey (C)
25g (1oz) each in pastel blue (D), lilac (E), pale beige (F), pastel pink (G), pale mauve (H), lavender (J), pale bleached green (L), pale rose (M), purple (N), palest blue grey (Q), salmon (R), light blue (S), mulberry (T), mauve-pink (U), maroon (V) and pale lime green (W)
1 pair each 2¼mm (US1) and 2¾mm (US2) needles
2¼mm (US1) circular needle

TENSION
31 sts and 39 rows to 10cm (4in) over chart patt on 2¾mm (US2) needles.
Note: Work colour patt by the intarsia method, see page 141.

SPECIAL INSTRUCTIONS
Work strawberry motifs following the instructions given on page 32, but work yarn T instead of W, A instead of B, and B instead of N.
Make bobbles following instructions on page 32.

BACK
Using 2¼mm (US1)needles and yarn A, cast on 143[151,159] sts.
Work in twisted rib as foll:
1st row (rs) K1 tbl, * P1, K1 tbl; rep from * to end of row.
2nd row P1, * K1 tbl, P1; rep from * to end.
Rep these 2 rows 20 times more, then 1st row again.

Next row Rib 2[6,10], * make 1, rib 7; rep from * ending last rep rib 1[5,9]. 164[172,180] sts.
Change to 2¾mm (US2) needles and beg colour patt from chart 1, working in st st unless otherwise indicated on chart, work 116[118,120] rows, ending with a ws row.
Shape armholes
Cast off 5 sts at beg of next 2 rows. 154[162, 170] sts. **
Now work 94[98,100] rows straight, ending with a ws row (when chart 1 is completed, cont in A only).
Shape shoulders
Cast off 17[18,19] sts at beg of next 4 rows, then 16[17,18] sts at beg of foll 2 rows.
Leave rem 54[56,58] sts on a spare needle.

FRONT
Work as given for back to **.
Now work straight until 187[191,193] chart rows have been completed, ending with a rs row.
Divide for neck
Next row Patt 71[74,77] and leave these sts on a spare needle, patt 12[14,16] and sl these sts on to a stitch holder, patt to end of row. 71[74,77] sts.
Cont on these sts only for left side of neck. Work 1 row.
Cast off 3 sts at beg of next and foll 4 alt rows.
Now dec 1 st at neck edge on every row until 50[53,56] sts rem (204[208,210] rows in all have been worked from chart 1).
Now work 10[12,14] rows straight, ending at armhole edge.
Shape shoulder
Cast off 17[18,19] sts at beg of next and foll alt row. 16[17,18] sts.
Work 1 row. Cast off.
With rs of work facing, return to sts on spare needle, rejoin yarn to next st, patt to end of row. 71[74,77] sts.
Complete right side of neck to match left reversing shapings.

This is the blue cotton version of the Basia sweater (as given in the pattern), a good spring and summer sweater. I've also worked it in wool and silks in lovely rich autumn colours, making an equally effective wintertime sweater.

BASIA CHART 1

A unless
otherwise
indicated

☑ B
☒ C
⊡ D
◪ E
◩ F
⊡ G
◮ H
⊟ J
◳ L
⊡ M
◭ N
⊤ Q
⊙ R
⊡ S
◥ T
⫼ U
⊞ V
◯ W

○ make
bobble
in colour
shown.

▨ make
strawberry
over
8 rows.

1st size back and front

2nd size back and front

3rd size back and front

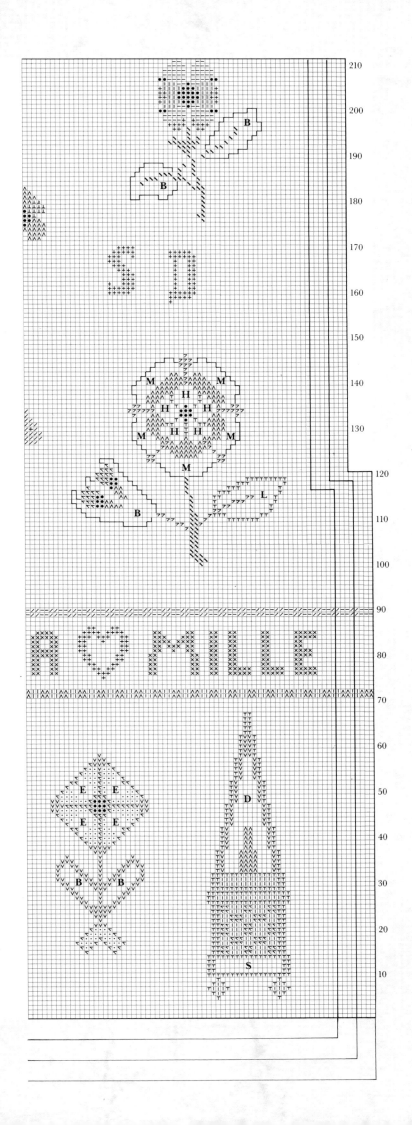

SLEEVES

Using 2¼mm (US1) needles and yarn A, cast on 67[69,71] sts.

Rib 43 rows in twisted rib as given for back of sweater.

Next row Rib 4[4,6], * make 1, rib 3; rep from * ending last rep rib 3[5,5]. 88[90,92] sts.

Change to 2¾mm (US2) needles and beg colour patt from chart 2, working in st st throughout, *at the same time* inc 1 st at each end of every 4th row until there are 164 [170,174] sts (when chart 2 is completed, cont in A only).

Work 2 rows straight.

Cast off.

COLLAR

Join both shoulder seams.

With rs of work facing, sl 6[7,8] sts off stitch holder at centre front on to a safety pin; and using 2¼mm (US1) circular needle and yarn A, K across rem 6[7,8] sts, then K up 33[34,35] sts up right front neck, K across 54[56,58] sts left on spare needle at back neck, K up 33[34,35] sts down left front neck, and K across 6[7,8] sts on safety pin (mark this point with a coloured thread). 132[138,144] sts.

Work in rounds.

Work in K1, P1 rib until collar measures 6·5cm (2½in), ending at marked point.

Work in rows.

Cont in K1, P1 rib until collar measures 12cm (5in) from K-up edge.

Cast off loosely in rib.

TO MAKE UP

Set in sleeves, easing to fit around cast-off sts at underarm.

Join side and sleeve seams.

BASIA CHART 2

FRUITS

Another of my favourites. I love the engravings from Elizabethan herbals where, in those early days of scientific observation, the urge for botanical accuracy can be seen vying with the urge for decoration. Embroiderers often used these herbals as source material for their stitchwork, producing wonderfully coloured and detailed work. In my own design I like the way the pattern fits the neat style of the garment so well, and I especially like the colours, which are tawny and subdued without losing their richness.

SIZES

To fit: 91[96,101]cm (36[38,40]in) bust
Actual width measurement: 96·5[101,106]cm (38¼[40,41¾]in)
Length: 55·5[57,58]cm (21¾[22½,23]in)
Sleeve seam: 42·5[43·5,44·5]cm (16¾[17¼, 17½]in)

MATERIALS

400[400,450]g (15[15,16]oz) four-ply wool in natural (A)
25g (1oz) each of dark brown (B), olive (C), dark green (D), gold (E), dark green fleck (F), pale mustard (G), grey-green fleck (H), pale yellow (J), aubergine (L), grey-brown (M), dark chilli (N), grey-green (Q), bottle green (R), light olive (S), red (T), olive grey (U), blue lovat (V) and midnight blue (W)
1 pair each 2¼mm (US1) and 2¾mm (US2) needles
2¼mm (US1) circular needle
2 buttons

TENSION

34 sts and 42 rows to 10cm (4in) over chart 1 patt on 2¾mm (US2) needles.
Note: Work colour patt by the intarsia method, see page 141.

BACK

Using 2¼mm (US1) needles and yarn A, cast on 143[151,159] sts. Work in twisted rib as foll:
1st row (rs) K1 tbl, * P1, K1 tbl; rep from * to end of row.
2nd row P1, * K1 tbl, P1; rep from * to end.
Rep these 2 rows 17 times more, then 1st row again.

FRUITS CHART 1

□ A unless
  otherwise
  indicated
Z B
T C
⊥ G
⊞ H
◣ J
◥ L
◩ M
◪ N
Ⅱ Q
⊡ R
⊡ S
◩ T
⊟ U
◪ V
⊠ W

*(Previous page)
Fruits photo-
graphed in
the drawing
room of a
Tuscan villa.*

Next row Rib 2[6,10], * make 1, rib 7; rep
from * ending last rep rib 1[5,9]. 164[172,180]
sts.
Change to 2¾mm (US2) needles and beg
colour patt from chart 1, working in st st
throughout as foll:
1st-4th rows Work in st st in A.
5th row K19[23,27]A, 1C, 30A, 2M, K to
end in A.
6th row P112[116,120]A, 6M, 14A, 6C, 5A,
2C, P to end in A.
These 2 rows set position of chart 1 patt.
Cont as set, work 106[108,110] rows, ending
with a ws row.
Shape armholes
Keeping patt correct, cast off 4 sts at beg of
next 2 rows, then dec 1 st at each end of foll
12[14,16] rows (131[137,143] rows have been
worked from chart). 132[136,140] sts. **
Work 71[71,69] rows straight, ending with a
ws row (when chart 1 is completed, cont in A
only).
Shape shoulders
Cast off 13[13,14] sts at beg of next 4 rows,
then 13[14,13] sts at beg of foll 2 rows.
Leave rem 54[56,58] sts on a spare needle for
collar.

FRONT
Work as given for back to **. Work 10[8,4]
rows straight, ending with a rs row.

FRUITS CHART 2

Divide for neck opening
Next row Patt 62[64,66] sts and leave these
sts on a spare needle, patt 8 sts and sl these
sts on to a stitch holder, patt to end.
62[64,66] sts.
Cont on these sts only for left side of neck.
Cont in patt as set, work 35 rows straight,
ending at front opening edge.
Shape neck
Cast off 4 sts at beg of next row, then 3 sts at
beg of foll 4 alt rows, then dec 1 st at neck
edge on next 7[8,9] rows. 39[40,41] sts.
Work 11[12,13] rows straight, ending at
armhole edge.
Shape shoulder
Cast off 13[13,14] sts at beg of next and foll
alt row. 13[14,13] sts.
Work 1 row.
Cast off.
With rs facing, return to sts on spare needle
at centre front, rejoin yarn, patt to end.
Complete right side of neck to match left
side, reversing shaping.

SLEEVES
Using 2¼mm (US1) needles and yarn A, cast
on 67[69,71] sts.
Work 37 rows in twisted rib as for back.
Next row Rib 4[4,6], * make 1, rib 2; rep
from * to last 3[5,5] sts, rib to end. 98[100,
102] sts.
Change to 2¾mm (US2) needles and beg
colour patt as foll:
1st-8th rows Work in st st in A, *at the same
time* inc 1 st at each end of 4th and 8th rows.
102[104,106] sts.
9th row K8[9,10]A, 2W, K to end in A.
10th row P51[52,53]A, 3W, 5A, 1W, 5A,
3W, 1A, 2W, 1A, 1W, 3A, 1W, 3A, 3W, 1A,
2W, 1A, 1W, 2A, 2W, K to end in A.
11th row K9[10,11]A, 1W, 3A, 1W, 4A, 1W,
2A, (1W, 3A) 3 times, 1W, 2A, 1W, 5A, 1W,
5A, 1W, K to end in A.
These rows set position of 'Prunus' motif on
chart 1.
12th-17th rows Cont as set, work 6 more
rows of 'Prunus' motif, *at the same time* inc 1 st
at each end of 12th and 16th rows. 106[108,
110] sts.
18th row P35[36,37]A, 5B, 18A, 1W, 3A, 1W
P to end in A.
19th row K42[43,44] A, 1W, 3A, 1W, 19A,
7B, K to end in A.
These 2 rows cont 'Prunus' motif and set
position of motif 1 from chart 1.
Cont as set until motif 1 is completed then

cont in A only, *at the same time* inc on every 4th row as before until there are 142[144,146] sts and 90 rows have been worked from top of rib, ending with a ws row.
91st row K15[16,17]A, 1C, 30A, 2M, K to end in A.
This row sets position of motif 2 from chart 1.
92nd-101st rows Cont to work motif 2 as set, inc on 92nd, 96th and 100th rows as before. 148[150,152] sts.
102nd row P51[52,53]A, 1W, 43A, 3B, 4A, 2B, 1A, 3R, 6A, 1R, 6D, 6A, 1D, P to end in A.
This row sets position of chart 2.
Cont to work chart 2 and motif 2 as set, inc on every 4th row as before until there are 164[170,172] sts.
Work straight until 148[152,156] rows have been worked from top of rib, ending with a ws row.
Shape top
Keeping patt correct, cast off 4 sts at beg of next 2 rows, then 3 sts at beg of foll 16 rows

(when motif 2 is completed, cont in A only). 108[114,116] sts.
Now cast off 10 sts at beg of next 6 rows. 48[54,56] sts.
Work 1 row.
Cast off.

BUTTONHOLE BAND
With rs of work facing, using 2¼mm (US1) needles and yarn A, K up from stitch holder at centre front as foll:
K-up row K3, make 1, K2, make 1, K3. 10 sts.
Work 15 rows in K1, P1 rib.
Make buttonhole
1st buttonhole row Rib 3, cast off 3, rib to end.
2nd buttonhole row Rib to end, casting on 3 sts over those cast off in previous row.
Rib 14 rows.
Rep 1st-2nd buttonhole rows.
Rib 4 rows, ending with a ws row.
Cast off 5 sts and leave rem 5 sts on a stitch holder.

BUTTON BAND
Using 2¼mm (US1) needles and yarn A, cast on 10 sts.
Work 38 rows in K1, P1 rib.
Cast off 5 sts and leave rem 5 sts on a stitch holder.

TO MAKE UP
Join both shoulder seams.
Sew left-hand row ends of buttonhole band neatly to right front opening.
Sew cast-on edge of button band to inside K-up edge of buttonhole band, so that cast-off sts are on left-hand side.
Sew right-hand row-end edge of button band to left front opening.
Collar
With rs of work facing, using 2¼mm (US1) circular needle and yarn A, rib across 5 sts on stitch holder at top of buttonhole band, K up 37[39,41] sts up right front neck edge, K across 54[56,58] sts from spare needle at back neck, K up 37[39,41] sts down left front neck and rib across 5 sts on stitch holder at top of button band. 138[144,150] sts.
Work in K1, P1 rib until collar measures 10cm (4in).
Cast off loosely in rib.
Set in sleeves.
Join side and sleeve seams.
Sew on buttons.

This page shows a detail from Fruits in the black colourway.

(Opposite) A leisurely breakfast on a vine-shaded terrace in the morning sun – the Garden cardigan in its cream colourway (as given in the pattern), and its black version.

Fantasy seems finally to have got the upper hand in these motifs: giant flowers sprout from tree-trunks; strawberries and lilies, chrysanthemums and honeysuckle grow from the same plants. It's the colours, though, that really make this design work for me; I wanted them to be subdued but still glowing, in the way that certain flowers will take on a particular incandescence in the fading light of dusk, as though they had absorbed the preceding hours' sunlight.

SIZES
To fit: 91[96,101]cm (36[38,40]in) bust
Actual width measurement: 101[106,111]cm (40[41¾,43¾]in)
Length: 66·5[68,69]cm (26¼[26¾,27¼]in)
Sleeve seam: 44[46,47]cm (17½[18,18½]in)

MATERIALS
425[450,450]g (15[16,16]oz) four-ply wool in cream (A)
25g (1oz) each in dark chilli (B), pale yellow (C), mauve pink (D), gold (E), pale orange (F), tangerine (G), lovat green (H), blue lovat (J), apricot (L), magenta (M), grey-brown (N), flecked grey-blue (Q), brownish pink (R), gentian (S), purple (T), dark brown (U), emerald fleck (V), slate blue (W), mid-blue (X), fuchsia (Y), pale blue (Z), grey-green (a), mid blue-green (b), maroon (c), peacock (d) and buttermilk (e)
1 pair each 2¼mm (US1) and 2¾mm (US2) needles
7 buttons

TENSION
33 sts and 41 rows to 10cm (4in) over patt on 2¾mm (US2) needles.
Note: Work colour patt by the intarsia method, see page 141.

BACK
Using 2¼mm (US1) needles and yarn A, cast on 147[155,163] sts.
Work in twisted rib as foll:
1st row (rs) K1 tbl, * P1, K1 tbl; rep from * to end of row.
2nd row P1, * K1 tbl, P1; rep from * to end of row.
Rep these 2 rows 18 times more, then 1st row again.
Next row Rib 4[8,2], * make 1, rib 7[7,8]; rep from * ending last rep rib 3[7,1]. 168 [176,184] sts.
Change to 2¾mm (US2) needles and beg in colour patt, working in st st throughout, as foll:
1st-4th rows Work in st st in A.
Now work in patt from chart 1, as foll:

5th row K2A, * 1R, 3A; rep from * to last 2 sts, 1R, 1A.
6th row (P3R, 1A) to end.
These 2 rows set chart position.
7th-24th rows Cont as set, work 3rd-20th rows from chart 1.
25th-38th rows Work in st st in A.
Now work in patt from chart 2 as foll:
39th row K13[17,21]A, patt 1st row of chart 2, K to end in A.
40th row P25[29,33]A, patt 2nd row of chart 2, P to end in A.
These 2 rows set position of chart 2.
41st-108th rows Cont as set, work 3rd-70th rows of chart 2.
** **109th-124th rows** Work in st st in A.
125th-144th rows Work 1st-20th rows from chart 1.
Work 2[4,6] rows st st in A, end ws row. **

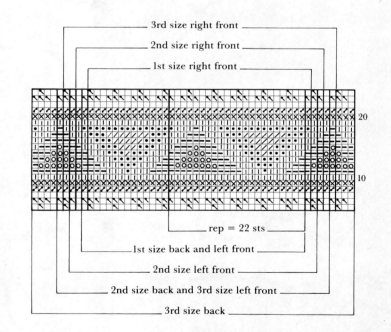

□	A
⊠	B
◨	C
⊞	D
◻	E
◩	F
◣	G
⊞	H
◤	J
◪	L
◨	M
◧	N
◿	Q
◺	R
◩	S
▼	T
◢	U
◨	V
◧	W
◨	X
◩	Y
◙	Z
⊞	a
⊡	b
◣	c
⊞	d
◻	e

GARDEN CHART 1

20

10

3rd size right front
2nd size right front
1st size right front
rep = 22 sts
1st size back and left front
2nd size left front
2nd size back and 3rd size left front
3rd size back

GARDEN CHART 2

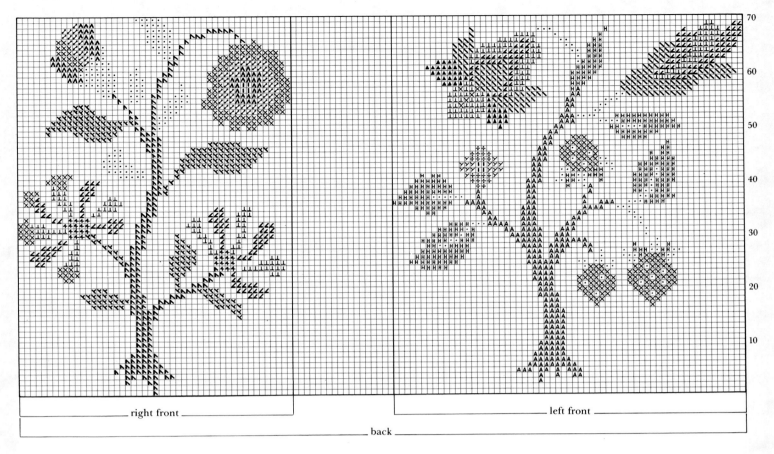

right front _left front_ _back_

GARDEN CHART 3

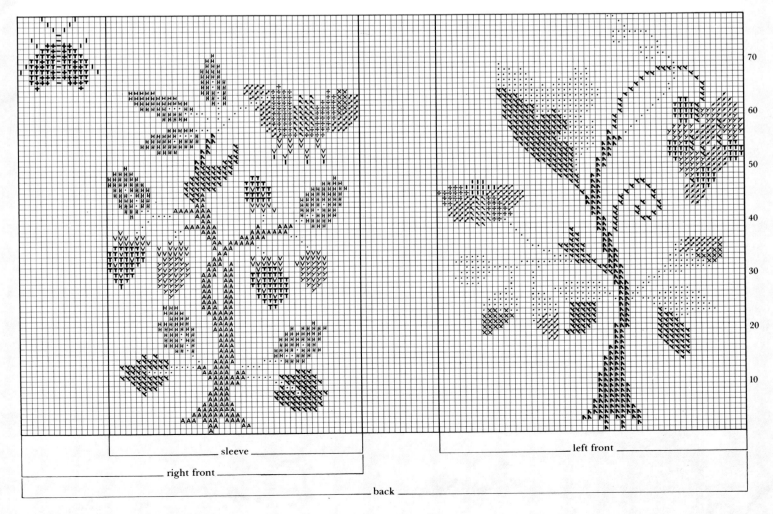

sleeve _left front_ _right front_ _back_

Shape armholes

Cont in st st in A.

Cast off 5 sts at beg of next 2 rows. 158[166,174] sts.

Work 11[9,7] rows straight (159 rows have been worked from top of rib).

Now work in patt from chart 3 as foll:

160th row P7[11,15]A, patt 1st row of chart 3, P to end in A.

161st row K19[23,27]A, patt 2nd row of chart 3, K to end in A.

These 2 rows set position of chart 3.

162nd-237th rows Cont as set, work 3rd-78th rows from chart 3.

Cont in st st in A, work 5[11,15] rows straight, ending with a ws row (242[248,252] rows have been worked from top of rib.)

Shape shoulders

Cast off 17[18,19] sts at beg of next 6 rows. Leave rem 56[58,60] sts on a spare needle.

LEFT FRONT

Using 2¼mm (US1) needles and yarn A, cast on 69[73,77] sts.

Work 39 rows in twisted rib as for back.

Next row Rib 5[2,4], * make 1, rib 6[7,7]; rep from * ending last rep rib 4[1,3]. 80[84,88] sts.

Change to 2¾mm (US2) needles and work in colour patt as foll:

1st-4th rows Work in st st in A.

5th-24th rows Work 1st-20th rows from chart 1 between left front markers. ***

25th-40th rows Work in st st in A.

Now work in patt from chart 2 as foll:

41st row K9[11,13]A, patt 3rd row of chart 2 between left front markers, K to end in A.

42nd row P8[10,12]A, patt 4th row of chart 2 between left front markers, P to end in A.

These 2 rows set position of chart 2.

43rd-108th rows Work 5th-70th rows from chart 2 between left front markers.

Work as given for back from ** to **.

Shape armhole

Cont in st st in A.

Cast off 5 sts at beg of next row. 75[79,83] sts.

Work 7[5,3] rows straight, ending at armhole edge (154 rows have been worked from top of rib).

Now work in patt from chart 3 as foll:

155th row K13[15,17]A, patt 1st row of chart 3 between left front markers, P to end in A.

156th row P6[8,10]A, patt 2nd row of chart 3 between left front markers, P to end in A.

These 2 rows set position of chart 3.

Cont as set work 63[67,69] rows from chart 3, ending with a rs row.

Shape neck

Keeping chart 3 patt correct, cast off 4 sts at beg of next row, and 3 sts at beg of foll 2 alt rows, then dec 1 st at neck edge on next 14[15,16] rows (when chart 3 is completed, cont in A only). 51[54,57] sts.

Now work 8[9,10] rows straight, ending at armhole edge (244[250,254] rows have been worked from top of rib).

Shape shoulder

Cast off 17[18,19] sts at beg of next and foll alt row. 17[18,19] sts.

Work 1 row.

Cast off.

RIGHT FRONT

Work as given for left front, working between right front markers on chart 1, to ***.

25th-38th rows Work in st st in A.

Now work in patt from chart 2 as foll:

39th row K10[12,14]A, patt 1st row of chart 2 between right front markers, K to end in A.

40th row P21[23,25]A, patt 2nd row of chart 2, P to end in A.

These 2 rows set position of chart 2. Cont as set, work 3rd-70th rows from chart 2.

Now work as given for back from ** to **.

Work 1 row, ending with a rs row.

Shape armhole

Cont in st st in A.

Cast off 5 sts at beg of next row. 75[79,83] sts.

Work 6[4,2] rows straight, ending with a ws row (154 rows have been worked from top of rib).

Now work in patt from chart 3 between right front markers as foll:

155th row K10[12,14]A, patt 1st row of chart 3, K to end in A.

156th row P6[8,10]A, patt 2nd row from chart 3, P to end in A.

These 2 rows set position of chart 3.

Complete as given for left front, reversing shapings.

SLEEVES

Using 2¼mm (US1) needles and yarn A, cast on 67[69,71] sts.

Work 39 rows in twisted rib as given for back.

Next row Rib 6[8,8], * make 1, rib 3; rep from * ending last rep rib 7[7,9]. 86[88,90] sts.

Change to 2¾mm (US2) needles and work in

The back of the black Garden cardigan.

colour patt as given for 1st-40th rows of left front but working between sleeve cuff markers on chart 4, *at the same time* inc 1 st at each end of every 4th row ending with a ws row. 106[108,110] sts.

Now work in patt from chart 3 between sleeve markers as foll:

41st row K28[29,30]A, patt 1st row of chart 3 between sleeve markers, K to end in A.

42nd row P32[33,34]A, patt 2nd row of chart 3 between sleeve markers, P to end in A.

These 2 rows set position of chart 3.

Cont as set until chart 3 is completed inc on every 4th row as before, ending with a ws row (118 rows have been worked from top of rib). 144[146,148] sts.

Work 4 rows in st st in yarn A, then work in patt from chart 4, working between sleeve top markers *at the same time* inc as before until there are 160[166,170] sts (when chart 4 is completed cont in A only).

Work straight until 150[158,162] rows have been worked from top of rib. Cast off.

BUTTON BAND

With rs of work facing, using 2¼mm (US1) needles and yarn A, K up 206[208,210] sts down left front edge from beg of neck shaping to cast-on edge. Work 10 rows in K1, P1 rib. Cast off in rib.

BUTTONHOLE BAND

With rs of work facing, using 2¼mm (US1) needles and yarn A, K up 206[208,210] sts

GARDEN CHART 4

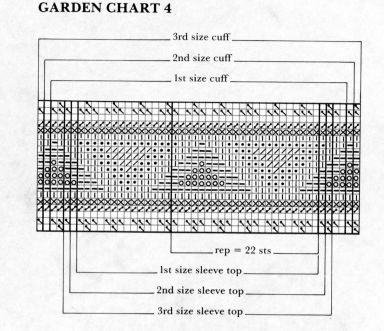

up right front edge from cast-on edge to beg of neck shaping.

Work 10 rows in K1, P1 rib making buttonholes on 4th and 5th rows as foll:

1st buttonhole row Rib 2[3,4], cast off 3 sts, * rib 30 sts including st used to cast off, cast off 3 sts; rep from * 5 times more, rib 3[4,5].

2nd buttonhole row Rib to end casting on 3 sts over those cast off in previous row. Complete as for button band.

COLLAR

Join both shoulder seams.

With rs of work facing, using 2¼mm (US1) needles and yarn A, K up 38[40,42] sts from halfway across top of buttonhole band up right neck edge, K across 56[58,60] sts on spare needle at back neck, K up 38[40,42] sts down left neck edge to halfway across button band. 132[138,144] sts.

Work in K1, P1 rib until collar measures 10cm (4in) from K-up edge.

Cast off loosely in rib.

TO MAKE UP

Set in sleeves, easing to fit around cast-off sts at underarm.

Join side and sleeve seams.

Sew on buttons.

□	A
⊠	B
◪	M
◲	Q
◸	R
⊟	W
◉	X
⊡	Z
Ⅱ	e

The detail shows the dark-grey colourway of the Garden design.

ROSES & RIBBONS

This is a quintessentially English design with its entwined roses, elegant and formal in a Regency style, perfect for picnics on well-manicured lawns on those English summer days when you wish you didn't need a pullover – but invariably do.

SIZES

To fit: 91[96,101]cm (36[38,40]in) bust
Actual width measurement: 95[100,105]cm (37½[39½,41½]in)
Length: 60[61·5,62·5]cm (23½[24¼,24¾]in)
Sleeve seam: 45·5[47·5,48·5]cm (18[18¾, 19]in)

MATERIALS

400[400,425]g (15[15,16]oz) four-ply wool in cream (A)
50g (2oz) each in dark purple (B), flecked grey-blue (C) and olive-grey (D)
25g (1oz) each in fuchsia (E), gold (F), lavender (G), grey-green (H), dark chilli (J), magenta (L), light blue (M), mauve pink (N), pink (Q), mid pink (R), blue-green (S), pale pink (T) and deep lilac (U)
1 pair each 2¼mm (US1) and 2¾mm (US2) needles

TENSION

33 sts and 42 rows to 10cm (4in) over patt on 2¾mm (US2) needles.
Note: Work colour patt by the intarsia method, see page 141.

BACK

Using 2¼mm (US1) needles and yarn A, cast on 143[151,159] sts.
Work in twisted rib as foll:
1st row (rs) K1 tbl, * P1, K1 tbl; rep from * to end of row.
2nd row P1, * K1 tbl, P1; rep from * to end of row.
Rep these 2 rows 20 times more, then 1st row again.
Next row Rib 2[6,10], * make 1, rib 7; rep from * ending last rep rib 1[5,9]. 164[172,180] sts.
Change to 2¾mm (US2) needles and beg colour patt from chart 1, working in st st throughout, as foll:
1st row (rs) K29[33,37]A, 1J, 5B, 1M, 4F, 2B, 1J, 77A, 1J, 2B, 4F, 1M, 5B, 1J, 30[34,38]A.
2nd row P30[34,38]A, 1J, 5B, 2M, 3F, 2B, 1J, 77A, 1J, 2B, 3F, 2M, 5B, 1J, 29[33,37]A.
These 2 rows set position of chart 1.
Cont as set, until 26 rows have been worked from chart 1.

Now beg patt from chart 1 and chart 2 as foll:
27th row K6[10,14]A, patt 1st row of chart 2, K6A, patt 27th row of chart 1, K7A, patt 1st row of chart 2 in reverse (reading from left to right instead of right to left), K6[10,14]A.
This row sets position of chart 1 and chart 2.
Cont as set until chart 2 is completed (43 rows have been worked from chart 1).
Now cont working from chart 1 only as before, working side sts in st st in A, until 76 rows have been worked from chart 1.
Now beg patt from chart 1 and chart 3 as foll:
77th row K6[10,14]A, patt 1st row of chart 3, K6A, patt 77th row of chart 1, K6A, patt 1st row of chart 3 in reverse (reading from left to right instead of right to left), K7[11,15]A.
This row sets position of chart 1 and chart 3.
Cont as set until chart 3 is completed (93 rows have been worked from chart 1).
Now cont working from chart 1 only as before, working side sts in st st in A, until 116[118,120] rows have been worked from top of rib, ending with a ws row.
Shape armholes
Keeping chart 1 patt correct, cast off 5 sts at beg of next 2 rows. 154[162,170] sts.
Now work straight until 126 rows have been worked from chart 1.
Now work in patt from chart 1 and chart 4 as foll:
127th row K3[7,11]A, patt 1st row of chart 4, K4A, patt 127th row of chart 1, K5A, patt 1st row of chart 4 in reverse (reading from left to right instead of right to left), K3[7,11]A.
This row sets position of chart 1 and chart 4.
Cont as set until chart 4 is completed (143 rows have been worked from chart 1).
Now cont working from chart 1 only as before working side sts in st st in A, until 176 rows have been worked from chart 1.
Now work in patt from chart 1 and chart 5 as foll:
177th row K3[7,11]A, patt 1st row of chart 5, K4A, patt 177th row of chart 1, K4A, patt 1st row of chart 5 in reverse (reading from left to right instead of right to left), K4[8,12]A.
This row sets position of chart 1 and chart 5.
Cont as set until chart 5 is completed.

(Previous page) A romantic photograph – just as it should be for this design. The background is in soft botany wool and for the contrast colours I used silks and Shetland wool – anything to get the right colours. It's also been made successfully in cotton.

This detail shows the way the small rosebud motif has been taken from the main design and repeated all over on the sleeve.

Now cont working from chart 1 only as before working side sts in st st in A, until 214[220,224] rows have been worked from chart 1, ending with a ws row.

Shape shoulders

Keeping chart 1 patt correct, cast off 17[18,19] sts at beg of next 4 rows then 16[17,18] sts at beg of foll 2 rows.

Leave rem 54[56,58] sts on a stitch holder.

FRONT

Work as given for back until 187[191,193] rows have been worked from top of rib, ending with a rs row.

Divide for neck

Keep patt as given for back correct.

Next row Patt 71[74,77] and leave these sts on a spare needle, patt 12[14,16] and leave these sts on a stitch holder, patt to end. 71[74,77] sts.

Cont on these sts only for left side of neck. Work 1 row.

Cast off 3 sts at beg of next and foll 4 alt rows, then dec 1 st at neck edge on every row until there are 50[53,56] sts.

Now work straight until 214[220,224] rows have been worked from top of rib, ending with a ws row.

Shape shoulder

Cast off 17[18,19] sts at beg of next row and foll alt row. Work 1 row.

Cast off rem 16[17,18] sts.

With rs of work facing, return to sts on spare needle, rejoin yarn to next st, patt to end of row. 71[74,77] sts.

Complete right side of neck to match left side, reversing shapings.

SLEEVES

Using 2¼mm (US1) needles and yarn A, cast on 67[69,71] sts.

Work 43 rows in twisted rib as for back.

Next row Rib 4[4,6], * make 1, rib 3; rep from * ending last rep rib 3[5,5]. 88[90,92] sts.

Change to 2¾mm (US2) needles and work 8 rows in st st, *at the same time* inc 1 st at each end of 4th and 8th rows. 92[94,96] sts.

9th row K18(19,20]A, patt 1st row of chart 2, K21A, patt 1st row of chart 2, K19[20,21]A.

This row sets position of chart 2.

Cont as set, *at the same time* inc on every 4th row as before, until chart 2 is completed.

Now work 23 rows in st st in A, inc as before on every 4th row (48 rows have been worked from top of rib). 112[114,116] sts.

Next row K8[9,10]A, (patt 1st row of chart 3, K21A) twice, patt 1st row of chart 3, K11[12,13]A.

This row sets position of chart 3.

Cont as set inc on every 4th row as before, until chart 3 is completed, then work 23 rows in st st in A (88 rows have been worked from top of rib). 132[134,136] sts.

Next row K38[39,40]A, patt 1st row of chart 4, K21A, patt 1st row of chart 4, K39[40, 41]A.

This row sets position of chart 4.

Cont as set, inc as before until chart 4 is completed, then work 23 rows in st st in A. (128 rows have been worked from top of rib). 152[154,156] sts.

Next row K28[29,30]A, (patt 1st row of chart 5, K21A) twice, patt 1st row of chart 5, K31[32,33]A.

This row sets position of chart 5.

Cont as set inc as before, until chart 5 is completed, then cont in st st in A only until there are 164[170,174] sts.

Now work straight until 154[162,166] rows have been worked from top of rib.

Cast off.

TO MAKE UP

Join right shoulder.

Neckband

With rs of work facing, using 2¼mm (US1) needles and yarn A, K up 33[34,35] sts down left front neck, K across 12[14,16] sts left on stitch holder at centre front, K up 33[34,35] sts up right front neck, then K across 54[56,58] sts on spare needle at back neck. 132[138,144] sts.

Work 6cm (2½in) in K1, P1 rib.

Cast off loosely in rib.

Join left shoulder and neckband seam.

Set in sleeves, easing to fit around cast-off sts at underarm. Join side and sleeve seams.

ROSES & RIBBONS CHART 1

110
100
90
80
70
60
50
40
30
20
10

beg chart 1 here

CHART 2   **CHART 3**   **CHART 4**   **CHART 5**

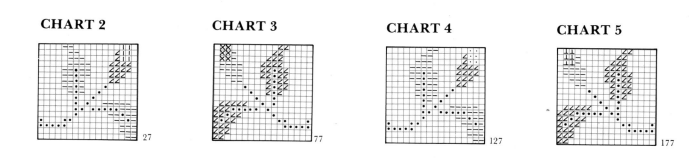

27   77   127   177

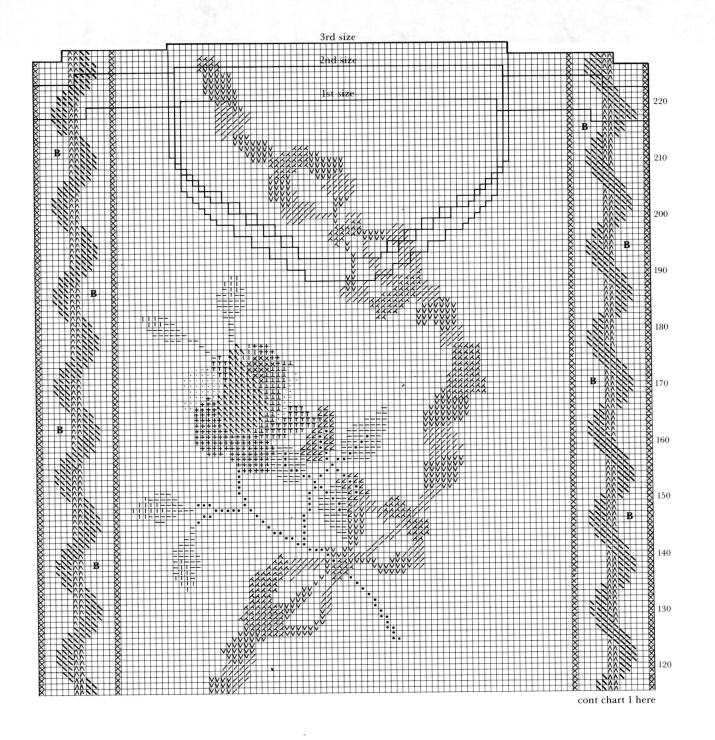

3rd size

2nd size

1st size

220

210

200

190

180

170

160

150

140

130

120

cont chart 1 here

A unless   C D E F G H J L M N Q R S T U
otherwise
indicated

TARTAN

The flowers in this design are based on an eighteenth-century Dutch still-life painting. As a knitwear designer I often find it very frustrating to see and appreciate paintings and know that in my own work I can't really get close to the subtlety, nicety of detail and nuance that can be achieved with paint on canvas. Nonetheless, this does make a very attractive knitwear design. I particularly like the way the soft blues of the tartan border contrast with the exuberant flowers above.

SIZES
To fit: 91[96,101]cm (36[38,40]in) bust
Actual width measurement: 104[109,114]cm (41[43,45]in)
Length: 63[65,66]cm (25[25¾,26]in)
Sleeve seam: 49[51,52]cm (19¼[20,20½]in)

MATERIALS
400[400,425]g (15[15,16]oz) four-ply wool in black (A)
50g (2oz) each in midnight blue (B) and light navy (C)
25g (1oz) each in mulberry (D), pink (E), purple grey (F), pale blue (G), warm purple (H), red (J), blue lovat (L), gold (M), blue-green (N), blue mist (Q), mauve pink (R), mid pink (S), magenta (T), gentian (U), dark chilli (V), pale pink (W), lovat green (X), pale peach (Y), olive grey (Z), buttermilk (a), fuchsia (b) and aquamarine (c)
1 pair each 2¼mm (US1) and 2¾mm (US2) needles
2¼mm (US1) circular needle

TENSION
33 sts and 39½ rows to 10cm (4in) over st st on 2¾mm (US2) needles.
Note: Work colour patt by the intarsia method, see page 141.

BACK
Using 2¼mm (US1) needles and yarn A, cast on 143[151,159] sts.
Work in twisted rib as foll:
1st row (rs) K1 tbl, * P1, K1 tbl; rep from * to end of row.
2nd row P1, * K1 tbl, P1; rep from * to end of row.

TARTAN CHART 1

rep = 50 sts

1st size back and front

2nd size back and front

TARTAN CHART 2

3rd size back and front

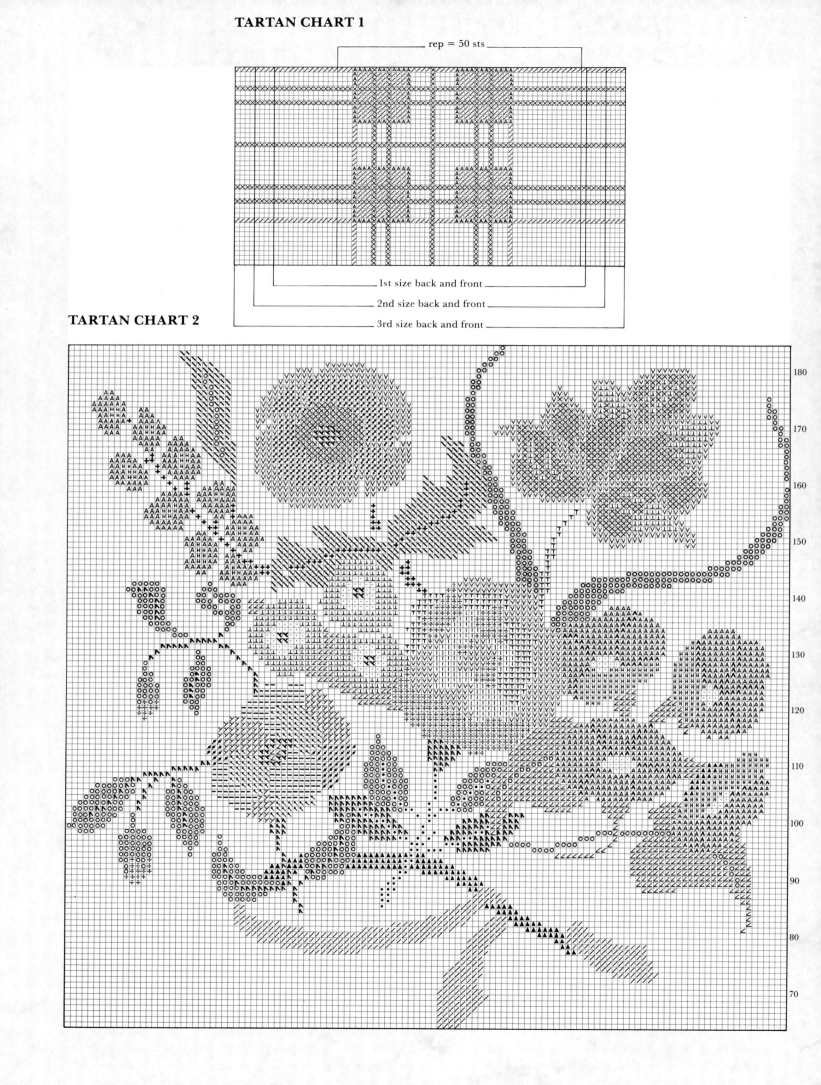

180

170

160

150

140

130

120

110

100

90

80

70

□	A
⊠	B
◩	C
⊞	D
⑴	E
⊡	F
◣	G
⊞	H
◹	J
◿	L
◥	M
◪	N
◿	Q
◩	R
◿	S
⊓	T
◭	U
◹	V
⊟	W
◉	X
⊠	Y
⊡	Z
⊡	a
◮	b
⊞	c

The photograph on page 96 was taken on the veranda of a palazzo in Lucca, a calm refuge from the heat and noise of the town.

(Right) The central motif in close-up.

Rep these 2 rows 20 times more then 1st row again.

Next row Rib 2[6,10], * make 1, rib 7; rep from * ending last rep rib 1[5,9]. 164[172,180] sts.

Change to 2¾mm (US2) needles and beg colour patt from chart 1, working in st st throughout, as foll:

1st row (rs) K1[5,9]A, * 14A, 1Q, 3A, 1B, 2A, 1B, 8A, 1B, 8A, 1B, 2A, 1B, 3A, 1Q, 3A; rep from * twice more, 13[17,21]A.

This row sets position of chart 1.

Cont as set work 2nd-42nd rows.

43rd-50th rows Rep 1st-8th rows.

51st row K to end in B.

52nd row P to end in A.

53rd row K5U[(3F,6U),(4C,3F,6U)], 3F, 6U, 3F, 8C, 3F, 7Q, 3F, 8C, 3F, 6U, 3F, 6U, 3F, 8C, 3F, 7Q, 3F, 8C, 3F, 6U, 3F, 6U, 3F, 8C, 3F, 7Q, 3F, 8C, 3F, 6U, 3F, 6U[(6U,3F,1C), (6U,3F,5C)].

54th row Work 53rd row in reverse but P instead of K.

55th row K to end in A.

56th row P to end in B.

57th-63rd rows Work in st st in A, beg and end with a K row.

Now work in colour patt from chart 2, working in st st throughout, beg with a P row, as foll:

64th row P80[84,88]A, 4Q, P to end in A.

65th row K79[83,87]A, 5Q, K to end in A.

These 2 rows set position of chart 2.

Cont as set until 116[118,120] rows have been worked from top of rib, ending with ws row.

Shape armholes

Cast off 5 sts at beg of next 2 rows. 154[162,170] sts.

Now keeping chart patt correct, work straight until 212[218,222] rows have been worked from top of rib, ending with a ws row (when chart 2 is completed, cont in A only).

Shape shoulders

Cast off 17[18,19] sts at beg of next 4 rows, then 16[17,18] sts at beg of foll 2 rows.

Leave rem 54[56,58] sts on a spare needle.

FRONT

Work as given for back until 187[191,193] rows have been worked from top of rib, ending with a rs row.

Divide for neck

Next row Patt 71[74,77] sts and leave these sts on a spare needle, patt 12[14,16] sts and leave on a stitch holder, patt to end. 71[74,77] sts.

Cont on these sts only for left side of neck. Work 1 row.

Cast off 3 sts at beg of next and foll 4 alt rows, then dec 1 st at neck edge on next 6 rows. 50[53,56] sts.

Now work straight until 214[220,224] rows have been worked from top of rib, ending with a ws row (when chart 2 is completed, cont in A only).

Shape shoulder

Cast off 17[18,19] sts at beg of next and foll alt row. 16[17,18] sts.

Work 1 row.

Cast off.

With rs of work facing, return to sts on spare needle, rejoin yarn to next st, patt to end. 71[74,77] sts.

Complete right side of neck to match left side, reversing shapings.

SLEEVES

Using 2¼mm (US1) needles and yarn A, cast on 67[69,71] sts.

Work 43 rows in twisted rib as for back.

Next row Rib 4[4,6], * make 1, rib 3; rep from * ending last rep rib 3[5,5]. 88[90,92] sts.

Change to 2¾mm (US2) needles and work in colour patt from chart 3, working between appropriate markers, as foll:

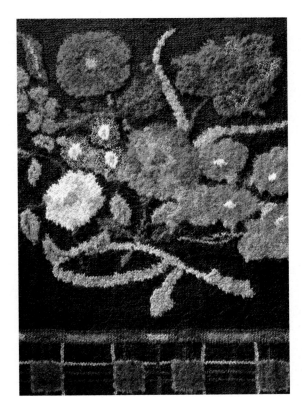

TARTAN CHART 3

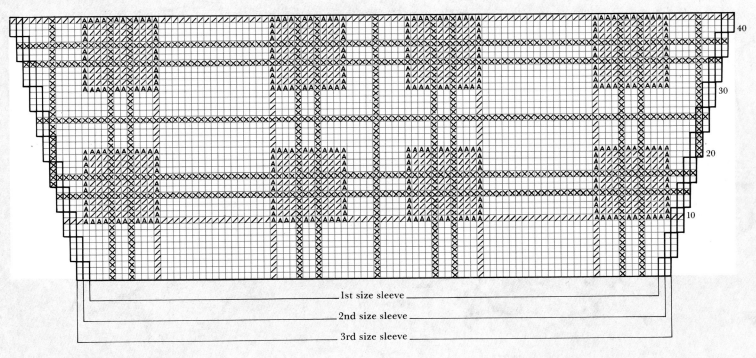

40
30
20
10

1st size sleeve
2nd size sleeve
3rd size sleeve

□ A
☒ B
☑ Q
▣ U

1st row (rs) K2[3,4]A, 1B, 2A, 1B, 3A, 1Q, 17A, 1Q, 3A, 1B, 2A, 1B, 8A, 1B, 8A, 1B, 2A, 1B, 3A, 1Q, 17A, 1Q, 3A, 1B, 2A, 1B, 3[4,5]A.
This row sets position of chart 3.
Cont as set, *at the same time* inc 1 st at each end of foll 3rd and then every 4th row until there are 108[110,112] sts working the incs into chart 3 patt. Work 2 rows straight (42 rows have been worked from top of rib and chart 3 is completed).
43rd row K3[4,5]A, * 1B, 8A, 1B, 2A, 1B, 3A, 1Q, 17A, 1Q, 3A, 1B, 2A, 1B, 8A; * rep from * to * once more, 1B, 4[5,6]A.
44th row With A, inc 1 P-wise in next st, P3[4,5]A, work from * to * of 43rd row twice but P instead of K, 1B, 2[3,4]A, inc 1 in last st. 110[112,114] sts.
45th and 47th rows K4[5,6]A, work from * to * of 43rd row twice, 1B, K5[6,7]A.
46th row As 45th row in reverse but P instead of K.
48th row With A, inc 1 P-wise in next st, P4[5,6]A, rep from * to * of 43rd row twice, 1B, P3[4,5]A, inc 1 P-wise in last st.
49th row K5[6,7]A, work from * to * of 43rd row twice, 1B, K6[7,8]A.
50th row As 49th row in reverse but P instead of K.
51st row K to end in B.
52nd row P to end in F, inc 1 at beg and end of row.
53rd row K3[4,5]F, * 7Q, 3F, 8C, 3F, 6U, 3F, 6U, 3F, 8C, 3F; rep from * once more, 7Q, 4[5,6] F.

54th row As 53rd row in reverse but P instead of K.
55th row K to end in F.
56th row P to end in B, inc 1 at beg and end of row. 116[118,120] sts.
Cont in st st in A only, *at the same time* inc on every 4th row as before until there are 164[170,174] sts.
Now work straight until 154[162,166] rows have been worked from top of rib.
Cast off.

COLLAR
Join both shoulders.
Using 2¼mm (US1) circular needle and yarn A, with rs of work facing, return to sts on stitch holder at centre front, sl next 6[7,8] sts on to a safety pin, K across 6[7,8] sts left on stitch holder, K up 33[34,35] sts up right front neck, K across 54[56,58] sts on spare needle at back neck, K up 33[34,35] sts down left front neck, K across 6[7,8] sts from safety pin and mark this point. 132[138,144] sts.
Work in rounds.
Work in K1, P1 rib until collar measures 6·5cm (2½in), ending at marked point.
Work in rows.
Cont in K1, P1 rib until collar measures 13cm (5in).
Cast off loosely in rib.

TO MAKE UP
Set in sleeves, easing to fit around cast-off sts at underarm. Join side and sleeve seams.

The main picture shows the back of Red Lion (page 126) with (from top left, anticlockwise) the back of the Millefiori waistcoat in fuchsia (page 133), Unicorn cardigan (page 120), Falconer (page 115) and Pairs (page 104).

PAIRS

Of all my designs this is probably my most enduring favourite. The design is adapted from nineteenth-century Danish wedding tapestries. These were specially woven to be used as double seat covers in the wedding carriage and would subsequently only be brought out on the most special occasions. Being wedding gifts, all the motifs come in pairs: two birds, a man and a woman, twinned flowers and so on. I love their quirky beauty, full of the detail that comes from familiarity with the things depicted but coming nowhere near a realistic photographic representation. The sweater has a neat, elegant style that looks equally good dressed up or down, for evening or daytime.

SIZES
To fit: 91[96,101]cm (36[38,40]in) bust
Actual width measurement: 106[111,116]cm (41¾[43¾,45¾]in)
Length: 62[63,65]cm (24½[24¾,25¼]in)
Sleeve seam: 46[47,48]cm (18[18½,19]in)

MATERIALS
400[400,425]g (15[15,16]oz) four-ply wool in cream (A)
25g (1oz) each in rust (B), pale mustard (C), grey-green (D), red (E), flecked fawn (F), bottle green (G), royal blue (H), mustard (J) mauve pink (L), lilac (M), oak brown (N) and turquoise (Q)
1 pair each 2¼mm (US1) and 2¾mm (US2) needles
2 buttons

TENSION
31 sts and 41 rows to 10cm (4in) over chart 1 patt on 2¾mm (US2) needles.
Note: Work colour patt by the intarsia method, see page 141.

BACK
Using 2¼mm (US1) needles and yarn A, cast on 143[151,159] sts.
Work in twisted rib as foll:
1st row (rs) K1 tbl, (P1, K1 tbl) to end.
2nd row P1, (K1 tbl, P1) to end.
Rep these 2 rows 20 times more, then 1st row again.
Next row Rib 2[6,10], *make 1, rib 7; rep from * ending last rep rib 1[5,9]. 164[172,180] sts.
Change to 2¾mm (US2) needles.
Work 8 rows in st st.
Now beg colour patt from chart 1, working in st st throughout, as foll:
1st row (rs) K14[18,22]A, patt 1st row of chart 1, K15[19,23]A.
2nd row P15[19,23]A, patt 2nd row of chart 1, P14[18,22]A.

These two rows set chart position. Cont as set until 96[98,100] rows have been completed from top of rib, ending with a ws row.

Shape armholes
Keeping patt correct, cast off 4 sts at beg of next 2 rows. Now dec 1 st at each end of next and every foll alt row until 124[128,132] sts rem.
Now work straight until 212[218,222] rows in all have been worked from top of rib (when chart patt is completed, cont in A only), ending with a ws row.

Shape shoulders
Cast off 10[11,11] sts at beg of next 4 rows, then 11[10,11] sts at beg of foll 2 rows. 62[64, 66]sts.
Leave rem sts on a spare needle for collar.

FRONT
Work as given for back until 151[155,157] rows in all have been worked from top of rib, ending with a rs row.

Divide for front opening
Next row P58[60,62] and leave these sts on a spare needle, P8 and sl these sts on to a stitch holder, P to end. 58[60,62] sts.
Cont on these sts only for left front shoulder.
Work straight until 187[191,193] rows have been worked from top of rib, ending with a rs row.

Shape neck
Cast off 4 sts at beg of next row, then 3 sts at beg of 5 foll alt rows.
Now dec 1 st at neck edge on foll 8[9,10] rows (206[211,214] rows have now been worked from top of rib). 31[32,33] sts.
Work 8[9,10] rows straight, ending at armhole edge.

Shape shoulder
Cast off 10[11,11] sts at beg of next and foll alt row.
Work 1 row.
Cast off rem 11[10,11] sts.

The cream colourway of the Pairs design. I really like the spicy reds of the flowers with old gold, royal blue, sky blue and violet detail. Though the pattern is inspired by Scandinavian themes, it looks quite at home in this flowery Italian meadow.

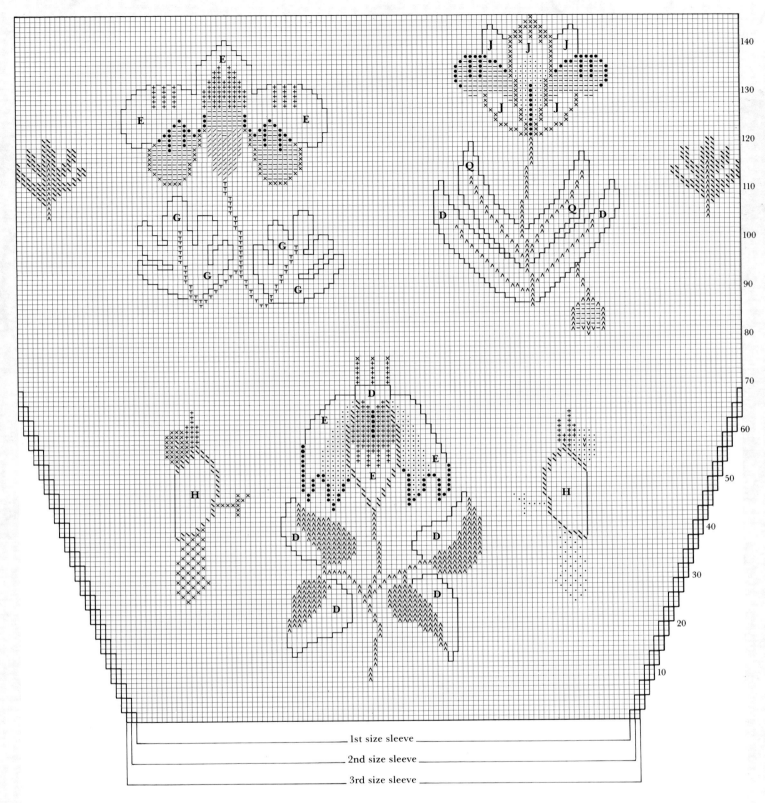

1st size sleeve

2nd size sleeve

3rd size sleeve

□
A unless
otherwise
indicated

⊡ Ⓐ ◿ ⊠ ⬤ ☑ ⊞ ⊟ ◩ ⊤
B C D E F H J L M N

Return to sts on spare needle and, with rs of work facing, rejoin yarn to inner edge, patt to end of row. 58[60,62] sts.
Complete right front shoulder to match left front shoulder, reversing shapings.

SLEEVES

Using 2¼mm (US1) needles and yarn A, cast on 67[69,71] sts.
Work 43 rows in twisted rib as given for back.
Next row Rib 4[4,6], *make 1, rib 2; rep from * ending last rep rib 3[5,5]. 98[100, 102] sts.
Change to 2¾mm (US2) needles and beg colour patt from chart 2, working in st st throughout, and in yarn A only when chart patt is complete, *at the same time* inc 1 st at each end of every 3rd row until there are 194[200,204] sts (144[150,153] rows have now been worked from top of rib).
Work 4[2,3] rows straight, ending with a ws row.

Shape sleeve top

Cast off 4 sts at beg of next 2 rows, then 3 sts at beg of foll 16[18,18] rows. 138[138,142] sts.
Now cast off 10 sts at beg of next 8 rows. 58[58,62] sts.
Work 1 row.
Cast off.

BUTTONHOLE BAND

With rs of work facing, using 2¼mm (US1) needles and yarn A, K up 10 sts from stitch holder at front neck as foll:
K-up row K3, make 1, K2, make 1, K3.
Work in K1, P1 rib as foll:
1st row (K1, P1) to end.
Rep this row 15 times more.
Now make buttonhole on next 2 rows as foll:
1st buttonhole row Rib 3, cast off 4, rib to end.
2nd buttonhole row Rib to end, casting on 4 sts over those cast off in previous row.
Rib 14 rows.
Rep 1st-2nd buttonhole rows.
Rib 4 rows, ending at opening edge.
Cast off 5 sts.
Leave rem 5 sts on a stitch holder for collar.

BUTTON BAND

Using 2¼mm (US1) needles and yarn A, cast on 10 sts.
Work in K1, P1 rib until button band measures same as buttonhole band to cast-off edge.
Cast off 5 sts.
Leave rem 5 sts on a stitch holder.

TO MAKE UP

Join shoulder seams.
Sew on buttonhole band, joining left-hand row ends to right front opening.
Sew on button band, matching cast-on edge to inside base of buttonhole band and with 5 sts on stitch holder at inside edge.
Collar
With rs of work facing, using 2¼mm (US1) needles and yarn A, rib 5 sts from buttonhole band stitch holder, K up 41[43,45] sts up right front neck edge, 62[64,66] sts from spare needle at back neck, and 41[43,45] sts down left front neck edge, then rib 5 sts from button band stitch holder. 154[160,166] sts.
Work in K1, P1 rib until collar measures 10cm (4in) from K-up row.
Join side and sleeve seams.
Set in sleeves.
Sew on buttons.

Here's a detail from the black colourway showing the stylized motifs – a woodpecker, an iris, a lily and the bridegroom.

TWO TREES

This style of garment – a classic waistcoat with pointed fronts and pockets – is one we've used often over the years. It can be worn by men or women, with trousers or skirts, over a shirt or next to the skin, or as a waistcoat really should be: underneath a smart suit jacket to give a little zest to an otherwise sober look. Being so adaptable, it can always be used in a fashionable way. The front of this waistcoat shows two 'Trees of Life'. The back takes the colours of the front and carries them around in stripes and geometric patterns. The idea of two completely different types of pattern in the same garment that nonetheless work perfectly together is very appealing to me and very satisfying to design.

SIZES

To fit: 96[101,106]cm (38[40,42]in) bust/chest
Actual width measurement: 100[105·5, 110·5]cm (39½[41½,43½]in)
Front length: 53[54·5,55·5]cm (21[21½,22]in)
Back length: 46[47·5,48·5]cm 18[18¾,19¼]in)

MATERIALS

250g (9oz) four-ply wool in black (A)
25g (1oz) each in blue lovat (B), pink (C), palest peach (D), light blue fleck (E), royal blue fleck (F), scarlet (G), sand (H), blue-green (J), rust (L) and pale mustard (M)
1 pair each 2¼mm (US1) and 2¾mm (US2) needles
4 buttons

TENSION

33 sts and 43 rows to 10cm (4in) over chart 5 patt on 2¾mm (US2) needles.
Note: Work colour patt by the intarsia method, see page 141.

BACK

Using 2¼mm (US1) needles and yarn A, cast on 145[153,161] sts. Work 7 rows in K1, P1 rib.
Next row Rib 3[7,4], * make 1, rib 10[10,11]; rep from * ending last rep rib 2[6,3]. 160[168,176] sts.
Change to 2¾mm (US2) needles and beg colour patt, working in st st, beg with a K row, as foll:
Work 2 rows in A. Work 15 rows from chart 1.
Now work 2 rows in A, 1 row in D, 2 rows in E, 2 rows in F, 1 row in D, 2 rows in A, 1 row in G, 2 rows in L, 3 rows in J, 3 rows in A, 2 rows in M, 2 rows in H, 2 rows in J, 1 row in A, 1 row in D, 2 rows in L, 1 row in J, 2 rows in A.
Work 8 rows from chart 2.
Now work 2 rows in A, 1 row in L, 2 rows in G, 2 rows in A, 1 row in C, 1 row in A, 2 rows in E, 2 rows in M, 1 row in A.
**Next row (ws) P16[20,24]G, 16C, 10E, 6M, 16G, 8C, 4E, 8M, 4E, 8C, 16G, 6M, 10E, 16C, 16[20,24]G. **
Next row As previous row but K instead of P.
Next row Rep from ** to **.
Now work 1 row in A, 2 rows in J, 2 rows in A. Work 8 rows from chart 3.
Now work 2 rows in A, 2 rows in F, 2 rows in D, 1 row in M, 2 rows in A, 2 rows in L, 1 row in F, 1 row in A, 2 rows in J, 2 rows in F.
Now work 86 rows from chart 4, *at the same time* shape armholes as foll: work 2[6,8] rows, then cast off 4 sts at beg of next 2 rows, then dec 1 st at each end of foll 9(11,13) rows, then dec 1 st at each end of next 9 alt rows. 116(120,124) sts.
Cont in A only, work 2[8,12] rows ending with a ws row.

Shape shoulders

Cast off 12[13,13] sts at beg of next 4 rows, then 13[12,13] sts at beg of foll 2 rows. 42[44,46] sts.
Change to 2¼mm (US1) needles and work 8 rows in K1, P1 rib. Cast off loosely in rib.

POCKET LININGS (make 2)

Using 2¾mm (US2) needles and yarn A, cast on 38 sts.
Beg with a K row, work 38 rows in st st. Leave these sts on a stitch holder.

LEFT FRONT

Using 2¾mm (US2) needles and yarn A, cast on 2 sts.

Shape front point

Work in st st as foll:
1st row (rs) Cast on 2 sts, K to end. 4 sts.
2nd row Cast on 3 sts, P to end. 7 sts.
3rd row Cast on 2 sts, K to end. 9 sts.
4th row Cast on 2[2,3] sts, P to end. 11[11,12] sts.

(Previous page) We photographed the Two Trees waistcoats in the famous Piazza del Campo in Siena, where once a year they hold a wild and dangerous medieval-style horse race. These waistcoats look great here worn with very smart suits.

TWO TREES CHART 4

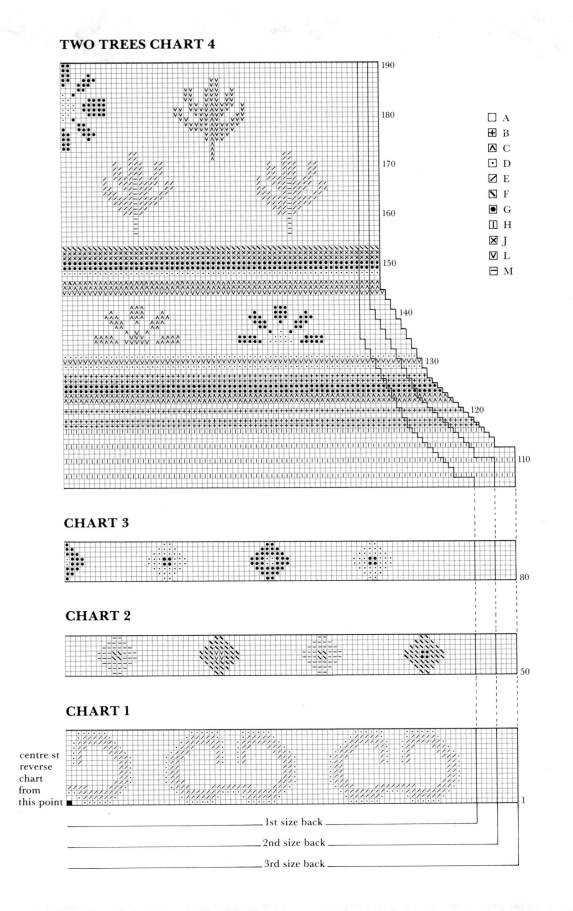

CHART 3

CHART 2

CHART 1

centre st
reverse
chart
from
this point

1st size back

2nd size back

3rd size back

A
B
C
D
E
F
G
H
J
L
M

TWO TREES CHART 5

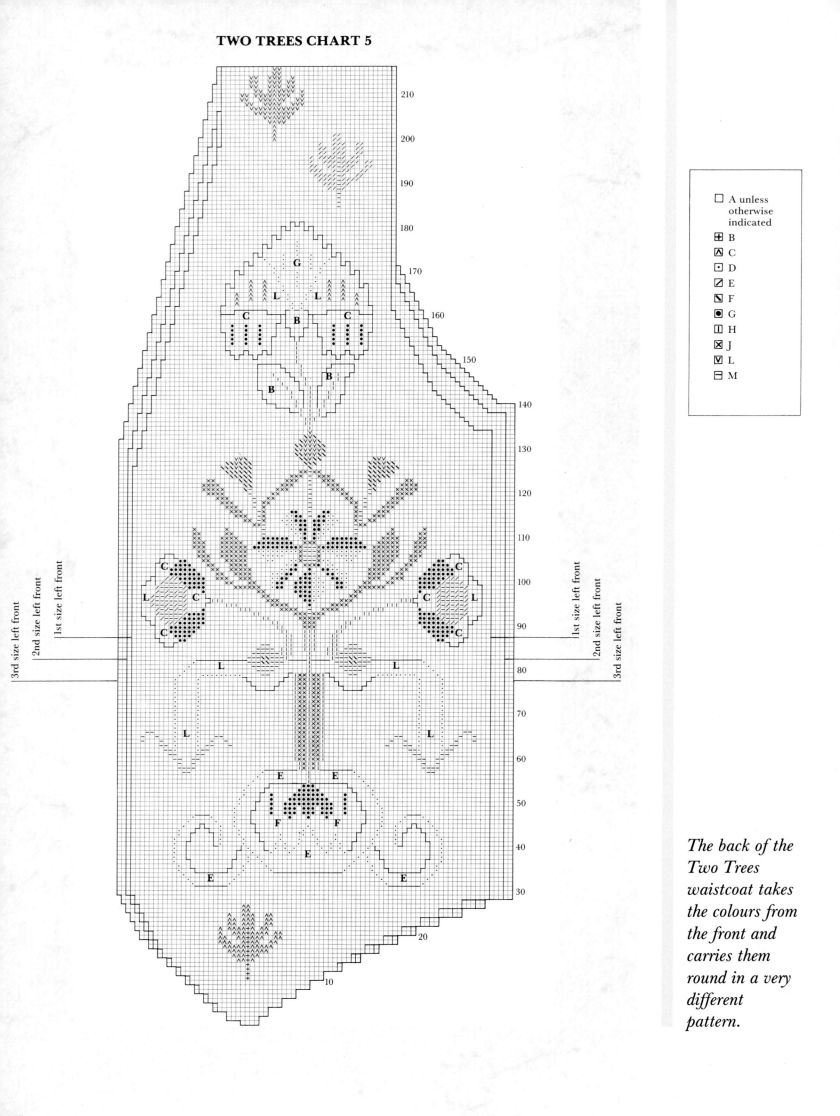

Key (right side):

- ☐ A unless otherwise indicated
- ⊞ B
- ◩ C
- ⊡ D
- ⊠ E
- ◳ F
- ◉ G
- ▯ H
- ⊠ J
- ⩒ L
- ⊟ M

Row numbers (right of chart): 210, 200, 190, 180, 170, 160, 150, 140, 130, 120, 110, 100, 90, 80, 70, 60, 50, 40, 30, 20, 10

Left labels: 3rd size left front, 2nd size left front, 1st size left front

Right labels: 1st size left front, 2nd size left front, 3rd size left front

The back of the Two Trees waistcoat takes the colours from the front and carries them round in a very different pattern.

Carry on in this way, casting on 3 sts at beg of K rows and 2 sts at beg of P rows until there are 26[26,27] sts.
Now beg colour patt from chart 5, working in st st and beg with 11th chart row, *at the same time* cont to shape point as foll:
11th row Cast on 3 sts, K16A, 1B, 12[12,13]A. 29[29,30] sts.
12th row Cast on 2 sts, P14[14,15]A, 1B, 16A. 31[31,32] sts.
13th row Cast on 3[3,4] sts, K19[19,20]A, 1B, 14[14,15]A.
14th row Cast on 2 sts, P16[16,17]A, 1B, 19[19,20]A.
15th row Cast on 3[4,4] sts, K21[22,23]A, 1C, 1B, 2C, 14[14,15]A.
16th row Cast on 2 sts, P15[15,16]A, 3C, 1B, 2C, 20[21,22]A.
Carry on in this way, cast on 3[4,4] sts at beg of next row, 1[2,2] sts at beg of foll row, 4 sts at beg of next row, 1[1,2] sts at beg of foll row and 4 sts at beg of next row. 54[57, 60] sts.
Now inc 1 st at beg of next row, cast on 4[4,5] sts at beg of foll row, inc 1 st at beg of next row, cast on 4[5,5] sts at beg of foll row, inc 1 st at beg of next row, cast on 5 sts at beg of next row, inc 1 st at beg of foll row, cast on 6 sts at beg of next row and inc 1 st at beg of foll row. 78[82,86] sts.
Keeping chart patt correct, work straight until 68 chart rows have been completed, ending with a ws row.
Place pocket
Next row Patt 20[23,25] sts, sl next 38 sts on to stitch holder, patt across 38 sts of pocket lining, patt to end. 78[82,86] sts.
Now work straight until 126[130,132] rows have been completed, ending with a ws row.
Shape front neck and armhole
Keeping chart patt correct, dec 1 st at front neck edge on next and 18[19,20] foll 4th rows, *at the same time* cast off 4 sts at armhole edge on 9th row (135th[139th,141st] chart row), and dec 1 st at same edge on foll 9[11,13] rows, then dec 1 st on same edge on 9 foll alt rows. 37[38,39] sts.
Now work straight until 222[228,232] rows in all have been completed, ending at armhole edge (when chart 5 is completed, cont in A only).
Shape shoulder
Cast off 12[13,13] sts at beg of next and foll alt row.
Work 1 row.
Cast off rem 13[12,13] sts.

RIGHT FRONT
Work as given for left front, reversing chart 5 patt, and all shapings.

POCKET TOPS (alike)
With rs of work facing, using 2¼mm (US1) needles and yarn A, rejoin yarn to sts left on stitch holder.
Work 6 rows in K1, P1 rib. Cast off in rib.

LEFT BUTTON BAND
With rs of work facing, using 2¼mm (US1) needles and yarn A, beg at left shoulder, K up 85[87,89] sts to beg of front neck shaping, K up 80[83,84] sts to beg of shaped edge, K up 36[37,38] sts to cast-on edge, K up 1 st from point and mark it, then K up 58[60,62] sts to left side edge. 260[268,274] sts.
1st row (P1, K1) to end.
2nd row (P1, K1) to marked st, make 1, K1, make 1, rib to end. 262[270,276] sts.
3rd-8th rows Carry on in this way, inc and working into rib 1 st at each side of marked st on 3 foll alt rows. Cast off in rib.

RIGHT BUTTONHOLE BAND
With rs of work facing, using 2¼mm (US1) needles and yarn A, beg at right side edge, K up 58[60,62] sts to cast-on edge, K up 1 st from point and mark it, K up 36[37,38] sts up shaped edge, K up 80[83,84] sts to beg of front neck shaping then K up 85[87,89] sts to shoulder. 260[268,274] sts.
Work as given for left button band making buttonholes on 4th and 5th rows as foll:
4th row Rib to marked st, make 1, K1, make 1, rib 37[38,39], cast off 2 sts, * rib 24[24,25] including st used to cast off, cast off 2 sts; rep from * twice more, rib to end.
5th row Rib to end, casting on 2 sts over each set of 2 sts cast off in previous row.
Work 3 more rows as given for left button band. Cast off in rib.

ARMBANDS (alike)
Join shoulder seams.
With rs of work facing, using 2¼mm (US1) needles and yarn A, K up 166[172,178] sts around armhole edge.
Work 7 rows in K1, P1 rib. Cast off in rib.

TO MAKE UP
Sew pocket linings to inside of fronts.
Sew down row ends of pocket tops.
Join side seams and armhole band seams.
Sew on buttons.

This is a great sweater for either men or women. It is substantial enough to be a good, practical outdoor sweater – but I have seen it look really good worn in the city as a mini-dress. The pattern is inspired by the Bayeux Tapestry which, aside from its historical value and the epic, compelling story it tells, is a beautifully composed and paced work of art with its lively and vivid detail, and its wonderful natural-dyed, tawny browns and reds now mellow and faded.

SIZES
To fit: 91[96,101]cm (36[38,40]in) bust/chest
Actual width measurement: 112[118,123]cm (44[46½,48½]in)
Length: 66[68·5,71]cm (26[27,28]in)
Sleeve seam: 42·5[44,45]cm (16¾[17½,17¾]in)

MATERIALS
600[600,625]g (22[22,23]oz) double knitting wool in black (A).
75g (3oz) each in chestnut (B) and mustard (C)
50g (2oz) each in palest green (D), pale blue (E), gold (F), pale grey (G) and mid blue (H)
25g (1oz) each in straw (J), red (L), natural (M) and dark grey (N)
1 pair each 3mm (US3) and 3¾mm (US5) needles

TENSION
25 sts and 31 rows to 10cm (4in) over chart patt on 3¾mm (US5) needles.
Note: Work colour patt by the intarsia method, see page 141.

BACK
Using 3mm (US3) needles and yarn A, cast on 125[133,139] sts.
Work in twisted rib as foll:
1st row (rs) K1 tbl, (P1, K1 tbl) to end.
2nd row P1, (K1 tbl, P1) to end.
Rep these 2 rows 3 times more, then 1st row again.
Next row Rib 6[4,6], * make 1, rib 8[9,9]; rep from * ending last rep rib 7[3,7]. 140[148,154] sts.
Change to 3¾mm (US5) needles and beg colour patt from chart 1 working in st st throughout as foll:
1st row (rs) K to end in A.
2nd row P to end in A.
3rd row K to end in J.
4th row P2[6,9]A, patt 4th row of chart 1, P2[6,9]A.
5th row K2[6,9]A, patt 5th row of chart 1, K2[6,9]A.
These 5 rows set position of chart 1.

Cont as set, beg and ending each row in A, except for 23rd, 26th, 44th, 47th, 69th, 72nd, 90th, 174th and 196th rows, where stripes should be worked from beg to end of each row.
Work 126[130,134] rows from top of rib, ending with a ws row.
Shape armholes
Cast off 4 sts at beg of next 2 rows (armhole shaping is not shown on chart). 132[140,146] sts. **
Now work straight until 200[208,216] rows in all have been worked from top of rib, ending with a ws row.
Shape shoulders
Cast off 14[15,16] sts at beg of next 4 rows, then 14[15,15] sts at beg of foll 2 rows.
Leave rem 48[50,52] sts on a spare needle, or cast them off for collar.

FRONT
Work as given for back to **.
Now work straight until 179[187,195] rows in all have been worked from top of rib, ending with a rs row.
Divide for neck
Next row Patt 61[64,66] and leave these sts on a spare needle, patt 10[12,14] and leave these sts on a stitch holder for neckband (or cast them off for collar), patt to end. 61[64, 66] sts.
Cont on these sts only for first side of neck.
Work 1 row.
Cast off 3 sts at beg of next and foll 2 alt rows, then dec 1 st at neck edge on foll 10 rows. 42[45,47] sts.
Work 6 rows straight, end at armhole edge.
Shape shoulder
Cast off 14[15,16] sts at beg of next and foll alt row. 14[15,15] sts.
Work 1 row.
Cast off.
With rs of work facing, return to sts on spare needle, rejoin yarn to next st, cast off 3 sts, patt to end.
Cast off 3 sts at beg of foll 2 alt rows, then dec 1 st at neck edge on foll 10 rows. 42[45,47] sts.

□	A unless otherwise indicated
⊤	B
⊠	C
⊙	D
◨	E
◩	F
⊡	G
⊘	H
☑	J
⊞	L
⊟	M
⊡	N

(Previous page) Looking north across the mouth of the river Arno in the evening to the Apennine mountains in the distance.

FALCONER CHART 2

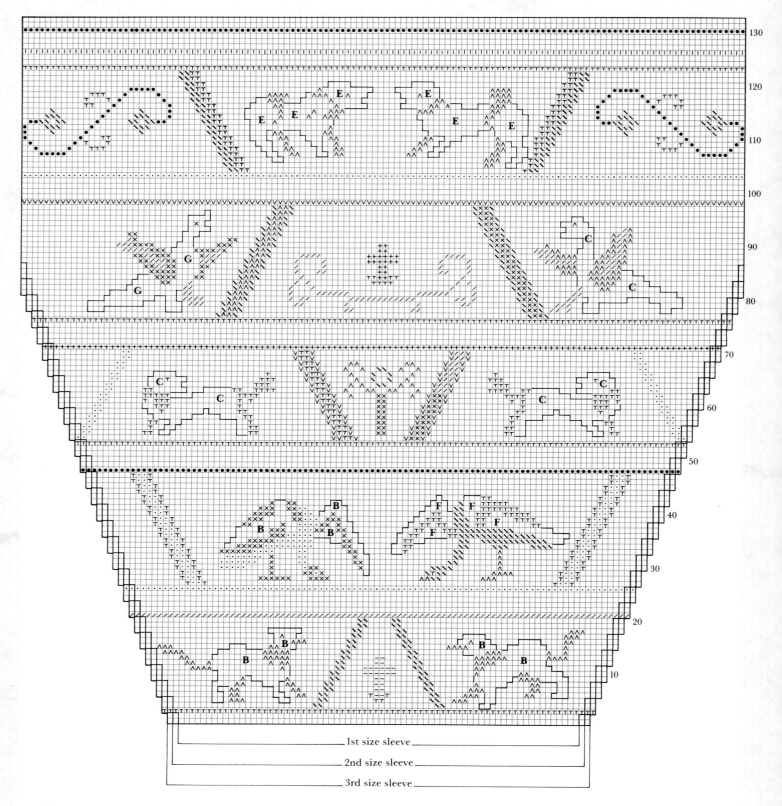

1st size sleeve

2nd size sleeve

3rd size sleeve

A unless
otherwise
indicated
B C D E F G H J L M N

Work 8 rows straight, end at armhole edge.
Complete as given for first side of neck.

SLEEVES

Using 3mm (US3) needles and yarn A, cast on 59[61,63] sts.
Work 9 rows in twisted rib as given for back.
Next row Rib 6[6,8], * make 1, rib 4; rep from * ending last rep rib 5[7,7]. 72[74,76] sts.
Change to 3¾mm (US5) needles and beg colour patt from chart 2, working in st st throughout, *at the same time* inc 1 st at each end of every 3rd row until there are 142[150,156] sts (105[114,120] rows have been worked from top of rib).
Work 19[14,12] rows straight.
Cast off.

COLLAR (optional)

Using 3mm (US3) needles and yarn A, cast on 118[122,126] sts.
Work in moss st as foll:

1st row (rs) (K1, P1) to end.
2nd row (P1, K1) to end.
Rep these 2 rows until collar measures 10cm (4in). Cast off.

TO MAKE UP

Join right shoulder seam.
If collar not required, work neckband.
Neckband
With rs of work facing, using 3mm (US3) needles and yarn A, K up 28 sts down left front neck, K 10[12,14] sts from stitch holder, K up 28 sts from right front neck and K 48[50,52] sts from spare needle at back neck. 114[118,122] sts.
Work 6 rows in K1, P1 rib.
Cast off loosely in rib.
Join left shoulder and neckband seam.
Sew on collar, if required, to neck edge so that row ends meet neatly at centre front.
Set in sleeves, easing to fit around cast-off sts at underarm.
Join side and sleeve seams.

Knitted in double knitting wool, this is a good, warm, practical sweater. Here it's shown in black, as in the pattern, and in a lovely, slightly beige cream. Over the years, and in an assortment of variations, this has been among our most successful designs.

UNICORN

I designed this after seeing the late fifteenth- or early sixteenth-century Unicorn Tapestries in The Cloisters museum in New York. There is, of course, no way one can accurately reproduce such works of fine art in knitwear; in fact there would be no point, as exact reproduction would leave no room for any input of one's own creativity. That said, if I've managed to catch the tiniest part of the magic feeling of those wonderful tapestries in this design, then I'm more than satisfied!

SIZES
To fit: 91[96,101]cm (36[38,40]in) bust/chest
Actual width measurement: 98[103,108]cm (38½[40½,42½]in)
Length: 58[59·5,60·5]cm (23[23½,23¾]in)
Sleeve seam: 44[45,46]cm (17¼[17¾,18]in)

MATERIALS
425[450,450]g (15[16,16]oz) four-ply wool in black (A)
50g (2oz) each in lovat green (B), blue green (C), oatmeal (D), pink (E) and mauve pink (F)
25g (1oz) each in gold (G), magenta (H), red (J), sky blue (L), oak brown (M), lilac fleck (N), grey brown (Q), mustard (R) and mushroom brown (S)
1 pair each 2¼mm (US1) and 2¾mm (US2) needles
6 buttons

TENSION
34 sts and 43 rows to 10cm (4in) over patt on 2¾mm (US2) needles.
Note: Work colour patt by the intarsia method, see page 141.

BACK
Using 2¼mm (US1) needles and yarn A, cast on 147[155,163] sts.
Work in twisted rib as foll:
1st row (rs) K1 tbl, * P1, K1 tbl; rep from * to end of row.
2nd row P1, * K1 tbl, P1; rep from * to end of row.
Rep these 2 rows 18 times more, then 1st row again.
Next row Rib 4[8,2], * make 1, rib 7[7,8]; rep from * ending last rep rib 3[7,1]. 168[176,184] sts.
Change to 2¾mm (US2) needles and beg colour patt from chart 1, working in st st throughout, as foll:
1st–4th rows Work in st st in A.
5th row K45[49,53]A, 1B, 37A, 1C, 84[88,92]A.
6th row P83[87,91]A, 2C, 36A, 3B, 44[48,52]A.

These 6 rows set position of chart patt.
Cont as set until 96[98,100] rows have been worked from chart, ending with a ws row.
Shape armholes
Cast off 5 sts at beg of next 2 rows. 158[166,174] sts.
Now work straight until 212[218,222] rows of chart have been completed, ending with a ws row (when chart 1 is completed, cont in A only).
Shape shoulders
Cast off 17[18,19] sts at beg of next 6 rows.
Leave rem 56[58,60] sts on a spare needle.

LEFT FRONT
Using 2¼mm (US1) needles and yarn A, cast on 69[73,77] sts.
Work 39 rows in twisted rib as given for back.
Next row Rib 5[2,4], * make 1, rib 6[7,7]; rep from * ending last rep rib 4[1,3]. 80[84,88] sts.
Change to 2¾mm (US2) needles and beg colour patt from chart 2, working in st st throughout. Work 96[98,100] rows, ending with a ws row.
Shape armhole
Cast off 5 sts at beg of next row. 75[79,83] sts.
Now work straight until 187[191,193] rows have been worked from chart, ending with a rs row.
Shape front neck
Cast off 4 sts at beg of next row, and 3 sts at beg of foll 2 alt rows, then dec 1 st at neck edge on next 14[15,16] rows (when chart 2 is completed, cont in A only). 51[54,57] sts.
Now work 8[9,10] rows straight (214[220, 224] rows have been completed from top of rib), ending with a ws row.
Shape shoulder
Cast off 17[18,19] sts at beg of next 2 rows. 17[18,19] sts.
Work 1 row.
Cast off.

RIGHT FRONT
Work as given for left front, reversing chart 2 patt and all shapings.

A back view of the Unicorn cardigan, the unicorn lost in a thicket of roses and periwinkles.

UNICORN CHART 2

A unless
otherwise
indicated

⊠ B
◣ C
☑ D
▨ E
◪ F
⊡ G
◿ H
॥ J
⊡ L
⊟ M
⊤ N
⊥ Q
⊞ R
◪ S

200

190

180

170

160

150

140

130

120

110

100

90

80

70

60

50

40

30

20

10

1st size left front

2nd size left front

3rd size left front

SLEEVES

Using 2¼mm (US1) needles and yarn A, cast on 67[69,71] sts.

Work 39 rows in twisted rib as for back.

Next row Rib 4[4,6], * make 1, rib 2; rep from * to last 3[5,5] sts, rib to end. 98[100, 102] sts.

Change to 2¾mm (US2) needles and beg colour patt from chart 3, working in st st throughout, *at the same time* inc 1 st at each end of every 3rd row until there are 196[202,206] sts (when chart 3 is completed, cont in A only).

Now work straight until 150[156,160] rows have been worked from top of rib.

Cast off.

BUTTON BAND

With rs of work facing, using 2¼mm (US1) needles and yarn A, K up 182[184,186] sts down left front edge from beg of neck shaping to cast-on edge.

Work 10 rows in K1, P1 rib.

Cast off in rib.

BUTTONHOLE BAND

With rs of work facing, using 2¼mm (US1) needles and yarn A, K up 182[184,186] sts up right front edge from cast-on edge to beg of neck shaping.

Work in K1, P1 rib as given for button band, making buttonholes on 5th and 6th rows as foll:

1st buttonhole row Rib 2[2,4], cast off 3 sts, * rib 32 including st used to cast off, cast off 3 sts; rep from * 4 times more, rib 2[4,4].

2nd buttonhole row Rib to end, casting on 3 sts over those cast off in previous row. Complete as for button band.

COLLAR

Join both shoulder seams.

With rs of work facing, using 2¼mm (US1) needles and yarn A, K up 38[40,42] sts from halfway across top of buttonhole band up right front neck edge, K across 56[58,60] sts left on spare needle at back neck, K up 38[40,42] sts down left front neck edge to halfway across button band. 132[138,144] sts.

Work in moss st as foll:

1st row (K1, P1) to end.

2nd row (P1, K1) to end.

These 2 rows form moss st patt rep. Rep these 2 rows until collar measures 10cm (4in) from K-up edge.

Cast off in patt.

TO MAKE UP

Set in sleeves, easing to fit around cast-off sts at underarm.

Join side and sleeve seams.

Sew on buttons.

□	A unless otherwise indicated
⊠	B
◩	C
☑	D
◪	E
◩	F
⬤	G
◩	H
⊡	J
⊡	L
⊟	M
⊤	N
⊡	Q
⊞	R
◩	S

The front of the Unicorn cardigan.

1st size sleeve

2nd size sleeve

3rd size sleeve

RED LION

Like Pairs, this design was inspired by Danish tapestries. The fronts and sleeves share flower motifs with the Pairs sweater while the back gets right away from that with one huge motif. I like the primitive drawing of the lion: very much a beast from a book of fairy tales rather than from a natural history text book and woven by people who had heard many stories about ferocious lions without ever actually having seen one. Designing this, I enjoyed shaking off the restrictions of working small repeat patterns, and doing something bold and not in the least understated!

SIZES
To fit: 91[96,101]cm (36[38,40]in) bust
Actual width measurement: 103·5[106,113]cm (40¾[42½,44½]in)
Length: 58[59·5,60·5]cm (23[23½,24]in)
Sleeve seam: 44[45,46]cm 17¼[17¾,18]in)

MATERIALS
425[450,450]g (15[16,16]oz) four-ply wool in royal blue (A)
75g (3oz) in dark blue fleck (B)
50g (2oz) each in slate blue (C) and black (D)
25g (1oz) each in emerald fleck (E), light blue fleck (F), red (G), mustard (H), scarlet (J), lilac fleck (L) and fuchsia (M)
1 pair each 2¼mm (US1) and 2¾mm (US2) needles
6 buttons

TENSION
31 sts and 43 rows to 10cm (4in) over chart 1 patt on 2¾mm (US2) needles.
Note: Work colour patt by the intarsia method, see page 141.

BACK
Using 2¼mm (US1) needles and yarn (A), cast on 147[155,163] sts.
Work in twisted rib as foll:
1st row (rs) K1 tbl, (P1, K1 tbl) to end.
2nd row P1, (K1 tbl, P1) to end.
Rep these 2 rows 18 times more, then 1st row again.
Next row Rib 4[8,2], * make 1, rib 7[7,8]; rep from * ending last rep rib 3[7,1]. 168 [176,184] sts.
Change to 2¾mm (US2) needles and work 5 rows in st st.
Now beg colour patt from chart 1, working in st st throughout, as foll:
1st row (ws) P16[20,24]A, patt 1st row of chart 1, P16[20,24]A.
2nd row K16[20,24]A, patt 2nd row of chart 1, K16[20,24]A.
These 2 rows set chart position. Cont as set

until 96[98,100] rows have been worked from top of rib, ending with a ws row.
Shape armholes
Cast off 5 sts at beg of next 2 rows. 158 [166,174] sts.
Now work straight until 212[218,222] rows have been worked from top of rib, ending with a ws row (when chart patt is complete cont in A only).
Shape shoulders
Cast off 16[17,18] sts at beg of next 4 rows, then 15[16,17] sts at beg of foll 2 rows.
Leave rem 64[66,68] sts on a spare needle for collar.

LEFT FRONT
Using 2¼mm (US1) needles and yarn A, cast on 69[73,77] sts.
Work 39 rows in twisted rib as for back.
Next row Rib 5[2,4], * make 1, rib 6[7,7]; rep from * ending last rep rib 4[1,3]. 80 [84,88] sts.
Change to 2¾mm (US2) needles and work 8 rows in st st, ending with a P row. **
Now beg colour patt from chart 2, working in st st throughout, as foll:
1st row (rs) K14[16,18]A, patt 1st row of chart 2, K18[20,22]A.
2nd row P18[20,22]A, patt 2nd row of chart 2, P14[16,18]A.
These 2 rows set chart position.
Cont as set until 96[98,100] rows have been worked from top of rib, end with a ws row.
Shape armhole
Cast off 5 sts at beg of next row. 75[79,83] sts.
Now work straight until 185[189,191] rows in all have been worked from top of rib, ending with a rs row.
Shape neck
Cast off 4 sts at beg of next row, then 3 sts at beg of foll 2 alt rows. Now dec 1 st at neck edge on next 18[19,20] rows (when chart patt is complete, cont in A only). 47[50,53] sts.
Work 6[7,8] rows straight, thus ending at armhole edge.

The Red Lion cardigan was photographed on a warm morning in front of the cathedral at Lucca. Though it looks great in a racy way here, I've seen it look just as stunning as part of a sophisticated city outfit.

RED LION CHART 2

RED LION CHART 3

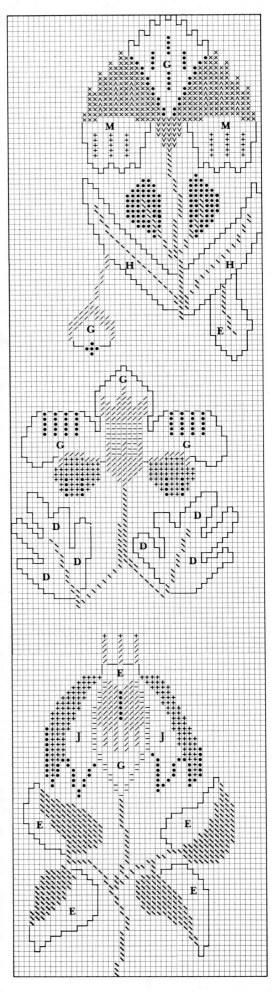

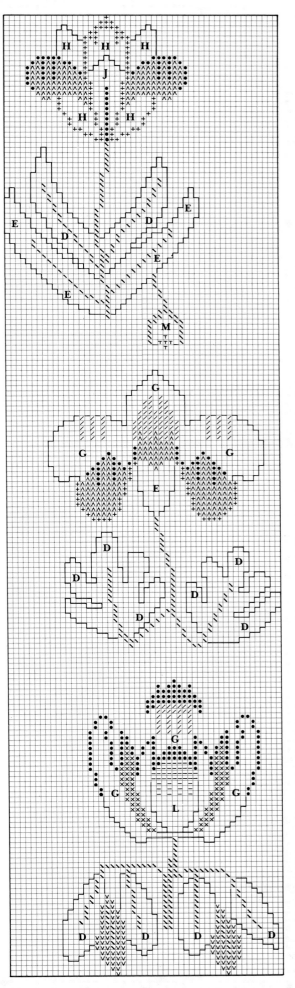

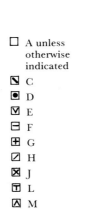

□ A unless
otherwise
indicated
◨ C
◉ D
☑ E
⊟ F
⊞ G
▨ H
⊠ J
⊤ L
◮ M

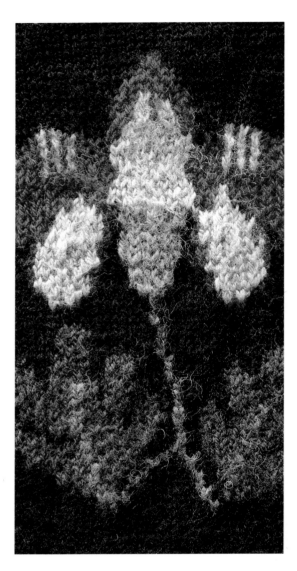

Shape shoulder
Cast off 16[17,18] sts at beg of next and foll
alt row. 15[16,17] sts.
Work 1 row. Cast off.

RIGHT FRONT

Work as given for left front to **.
Now beg colour patt from chart 3, working in
st st throughout as foll:
1st row (rs) K15[17,19]A, patt 1st row of
chart 3, K13[15,17]A.
2nd row P13[15,17]A, patt 2nd row of chart
3, P15[17,19]A.
These 2 rows set chart position.
Complete to match left front, reversing
shapings.

SLEEVES

Using 2¼mm (US1) needles and yarn A, cast
on 67[69,71] sts.

Work 39 rows in twisted rib as for back.
Next row Rib 4[4,6], * make 1, rib 2; rep
from * ending last rep rib 3[5,5]. 98[100,102]
sts.
Change to 2¾mm (US2) needles and beg
colour patt from chart 4, working in st st
throughout, *at the same time* inc 1 st at each
end of every 3rd row until there are
196[202,206] sts, working the incs in A (and
when chart 4 is complete, cont in A only).
Work straight until 150[156,160] rows in all
have been worked from top of rib.
Cast off.

BUTTON BAND

With rs of work facing, using 2¼mm (US1)
needles and yarn A, K up 182[184,186] sts
evenly down left front edge from beg of neck
shaping to cast-on edge.
Work 10 rows in K1, P1 rib.
Cast off in rib.

BUTTONHOLE BAND

With rs facing, using 2¼mm (US1) needles
and yarn A, K up 182[184,186] sts evenly up
right front edge from cast-on edge to beg of
neck shaping.
Work 4 rows in K1, P1 rib.
1st buttonhole row Rib 2[2,4], cast off 3 sts,
* rib 32 including st used to cast off, cast off
3 sts; rep from * to last 2[4,4] sts, rib to end
of row.
2nd buttonhole row Rib to end, casting on
3 sts over those cast off in previous row.
Rib 4 rows.
Cast off in rib.

TO MAKE UP

Join shoulder seams.
Collar
With rs of work facing, using 2¼mm (US1)
needles and yarn A, K up 42[44,46] sts
evenly from halfway across buttonhole band
to shoulder seam, K across 64[66,68] sts on
spare needle at back neck, then K up
42[44,46] sts down left front neck to halfway
across button band. 148[154,160] sts.
Work in moss st as foll:
1st row (K1, P1) to end.
2nd row (P1, K1) to end.
Rep these 2 rows until collar measures 10cm
(4in) from K-up edge.
Set in sleeves, easing to fit around cast-off sts
at underarm.
Join side and sleeve seams.
Sew on buttons.

*The detail
shows the front
of the Red Lion
cardigan.*

RED LION CHART 4

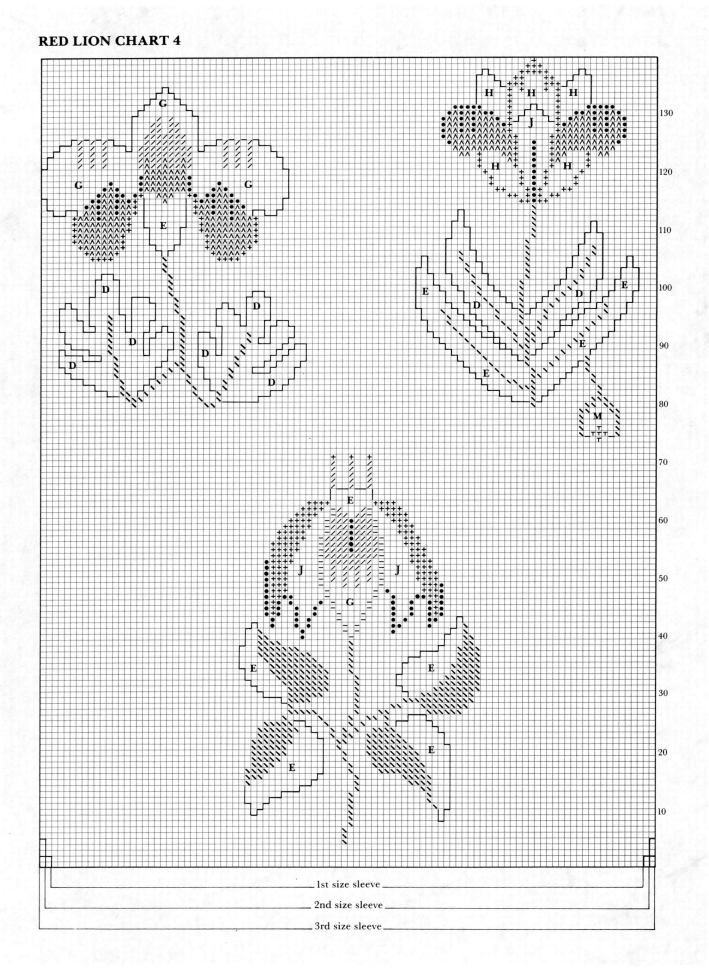

130

120

110

100

90

80

70

60

50

40

30

20

10

1st size sleeve

2nd size sleeve

3rd size sleeve

A unless   C D E F G H J L M
otherwise
indicated

MILLEFIORI CHART 1

1st size back
2nd size back
3rd size back
4th size back

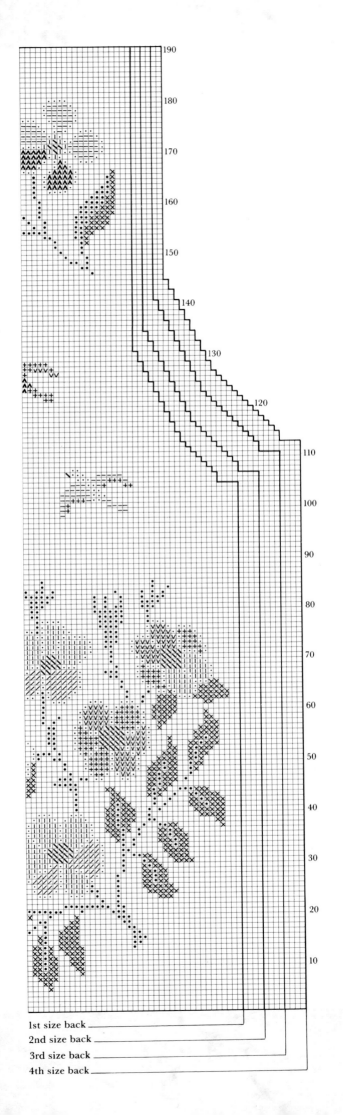

1st size back

2nd size back

3rd size back

4th size back

'Millefiori' means 'a thousand flowers'. The backgrounds of many Italian and French medieval tapestries are adorned with millefiori designs in which many different types of flower are depicted vividly, delicately and in great abundance.

SIZES

To fit: 91[96,101,106]cm (36[38,40,42]in) bust/chest
Actual width measurement: 93[98,103, 108]cm (36½[38½,40½,42½]in)
Back length: 47[48,50·5,51]cm (18½[19, 19¾,20]in)

MATERIALS

225[250,250,250]g (8[9,9,9]oz) four-ply wool in magenta (A)
50g (2oz) each in slate blue (B), emerald fleck (C) and dove grey (D)
25g (1oz) each in pink (E), scarlet (F), gold (G), orange-pink (H), red (J), lilac fleck (L) and iris (M)
1 pair each 2¼mm (US1) and 2¾mm (US2) needles
4 buttons

TENSION

33 sts and 41 rows to 10cm (4in) over patt on 2¾mm (US2) needles.
Note: Work colour patt by the intarsia method, see page 141.

BACK

Using 2¼mm (US1) needles and yarn A, cast on 137[145,153,161] sts.
Work in K1, P1 rib as foll:
1st row (rs) (K1, P1) to last st, K1.
2nd row (P1, K1) to last st, P1.
Rep these 2 rows twice more, then 1st row again.
Next row Rib 6[3,7,4], * make 1, rib 9[10,10,11]; rep from * ending last rep rib 5[2,6,3]. 152[160,168,176] sts.
Change to 2¾mm (US2) needles and beg colour patt from chart 1, working in st st throughout, work 104[106,110,112] rows, ending with a ws row.
Shape armholes
Keeping patt correct, cast off 4 sts at beg of next 2 rows, then dec 1 st at each end of foll 7[9,11,13] rows.

MILLEFIORI CHART 3

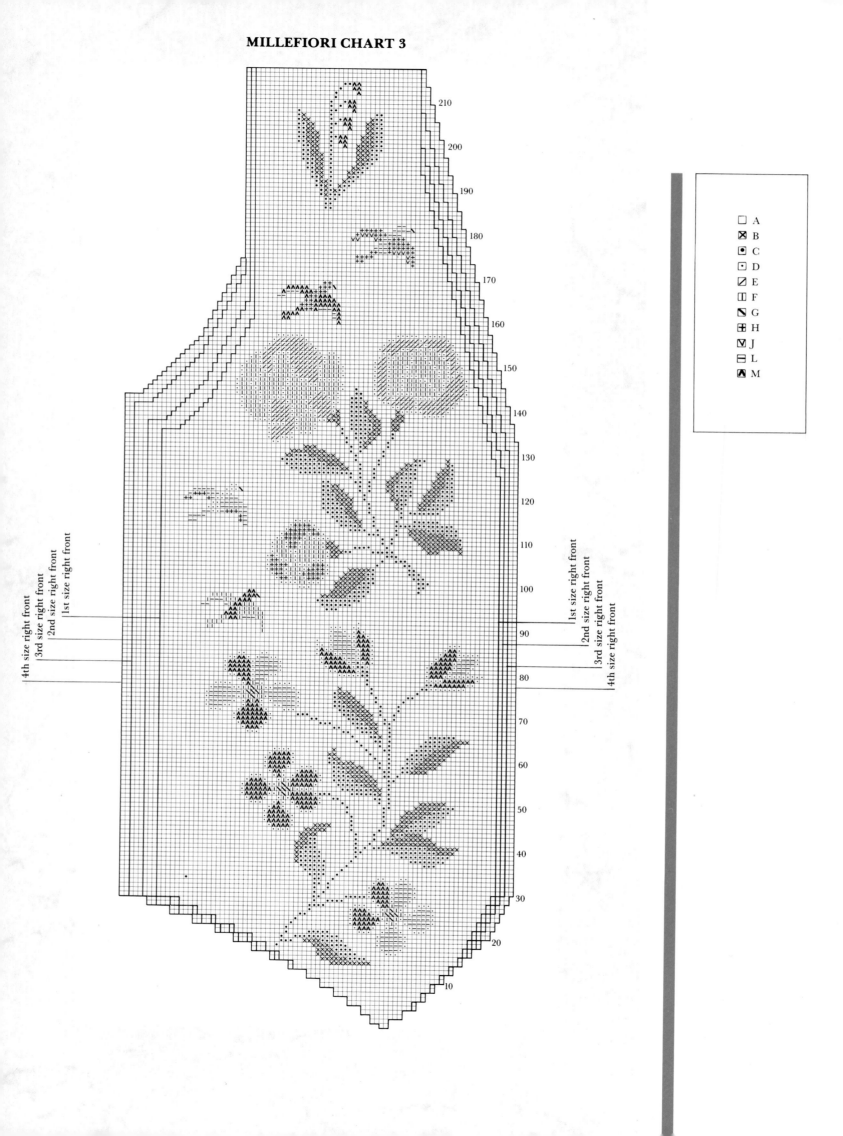

210
200
190
180
170
160
150
140
130
120
110
100
90
80
70
60
50
40
30
20
10

4th size right front
3rd size right front
2nd size right front
1st size right front

1st size right front
2nd size right front
3rd size right front
4th size right front

☐ A
⊠ B
⊙ C
⊡ D
◪ E
⊞ F
◩ G
⊞ H
◪ J
⊟ L
◪ M

MILLEFIORI CHART 2

4th size left front
3rd size left front
2nd size left front
1st size left front

1st size left front
2nd size left front
3rd size left front
4th size left front

10
20
30
40
50
60
70
80
90
100
110
120
130
140
150
160
170
180
190
200
210

Now dec 1 st at each end of foll 9 alt rows (131[135,141,145] chart rows have been completed). 112[116,120,124] sts.
Work 57 rows straight, end with ws row.

Shape shoulders
Cast off 12[12,13,13] sts at beg of next 4 rows, then cast off 12[13,12,13] sts at beg of next 2 rows. 40[42,44,46] sts.
Change to 2¼mm (US1) needles and work 8 rows in K1, P1 rib in yarn A.
Cast off loosely in rib.

LEFT FRONT
Using 2¾mm (US2) needles and yarn A, cast on 2 sts.
1st row P2.

Shape front point
Next row Cast on 2 sts, K to end. 4 sts.
Next row Cast on 3 sts, P to end. 7 sts.
Next row Cast on 2 sts, K to end. 9 sts.
Next row Cast on 2[2,2,3] sts, P to end. 11[11,11,12] sts.
** **Next row** Cast on 3 sts, K to end.
Next row Cast on 2 sts, P to end. **
Rep from ** to ** 3 times more. 31[31,31,32] sts.
Next row Cast on 3[3,3,4] sts, K to end. 34[34,34,36] sts.
Now beg colour patt from chart 2, beg with 15th row as foll:
15th row With A, cast on 2 sts, P18[18,18,19]A, 1B, 17[17,17,18]A. 36[36,36,38] sts.
16th row With A, cast on 3[3,4,4] sts, K20[20,21,22]A, 2B, 17[17,17,18]A.
These 2 rows set chart position.
Keeping chart patt correct, cont to shape point as foll:
17th row Cast on 1[2,2,2] sts, patt to end.
18th row Cast on 3[3,4,4] sts, patt to end.
19th row Cast on 1[1,2,2] sts, patt to end.
20th row Cast on 3[4,4,4] sts, patt to end.
21st row Cast on 1[1,1,2] sts, patt to end.
22nd row Cast on 4 sts, patt to end.
23rd row Inc 1, patt to end. 53[55,58,61] sts.
24th row Cast on 4[4,4,5] sts, patt to end.
25th row As 23rd row.
26th row Cast on 4[4,5,5] sts, patt to end.
27th row As 23rd row.
28th row Cast on 4[5,5,5] sts patt to end.
29th row As 23rd row.
30th row Cast on 5[6,6,6] sts, patt to end.
31st row As 23rd row. 74[78,82,86] sts.
Now work straight, foll chart patt as set, until 125th[127th,131st,133rd] chart row has been completed, ending with a P row.

Shape front neck
Keeping patt correct, dec 1 st at neck edge on next and every foll 4th row until 71[75,79,83] sts rem, ending with a P row. ***

Shape armhole
Cont to dec for front neck on every 4th row as set, *at the same time* cast off 4 sts at beg of next row, then dec 1 st at armhole edge on foll 7[9,11,13] rows, then on same edge on foll 9 alt rows. 45[46,48,49] sts.
Cont to dec on front neck edge as set until 36[37,38,39] sts rem.
Now work 23[21,19,17] rows straight (when chart 2 is completed, cont in A only), ending at armhole edge.

Shape shoulder
Cast off 12[12,13,13] sts at beg of next and foll alt row. 12[13,12,13] sts.
Work 1 row.
Cast off.

RIGHT FRONT
Work as given for left front to ***, reversing all shapings and working from chart 3 instead of chart 2.
Work 1 row.
Complete to match left front.

BUTTON BAND
With rs of work facing, using 2¼mm (US1) needles and yarn A, K up 83[85,87,89] sts from cast-off edge of left front down to beg of front neck shaping, K up 79[80,83,84] sts to beg of front point shaping, K up 35[36,37,38] sts to point, K up 1 st from point and mark this st, K up 56[58,60,62] sts to left side edge. 254[260,268,274] sts.
Work in K1, P1 rib as foll:
Next row (P1, K1) to end.
Next row Rib to marked st, make 1, K1, make 1, rib to end.
Next row Rib to end.
Rep last 2 rows twice more then first row again. 262[268,276,282] sts.
Cast off loosely in rib.

BUTTONHOLE BAND
With rs of work facing, using 2¼mm (US1) needles and yarn A, K up 56[58,60,62] sts from right side edge of right front down to point, K up 1 st from point and mark this st, K up 35[36,37,38] sts up shaped edge to end of point shaping, K up 79[80,83,84] sts up to beg of front neck shaping, and K up 83[85,87,89] sts to cast-off edge. 254[260,268,274] sts.

The colourway given in the pattern is the magenta shown on page 133. The one opposite is a cream version.

Work in K1, P1 rib as given for button band, making buttonholes on 4th and 5th rows as foll:

1st buttonhole row Rib to marked st, make 1, K1, make 1, rib 36[37,38,39], cast off 2 sts, * rib 23[24,25,25], cast off 2 sts; rep from * twice more, rib to end.

2nd buttonhole row Rib to end casting on 2 sts over 2 sts cast off in previous row. Complete as given for button band.

ARMBANDS
Join shoulder seams.
With rs of work facing, using 2¼mm (US1) needles and yarn A, K up 162[166,172,178] sts evenly around armhole edge.
Work 7 rows in K1, P1 rib. Cast off in rib.

TO MAKE UP
Join side and armhole seams.
Sew on buttons.

READING THE PATTERNS

Most of the patterns in the book are quite straightforward. There are very few stitch patterns other than stocking stitch and rib, just the occasional fancy stitch or bobble, and a little reversed stocking stitch, so they should be well within the capabilities of most averagely good knitters.

SIZES

Many of the patterns provide instructions for several sizes. The smallest size is given first, with the larger sizes following in square brackets. Both the *actual* measurements and the *to fit* measurement are specified for each garment, and the former are always larger than the latter, the amount varying depending on whether a sweater is intended to be neat and close-fitting or loose and baggy. Look at the actual as well as the to fit measurement when deciding which size you wish to knit. In the course of the pattern, where only one set of instructions is given, it applies to all sizes; where the instructions for the different sizes vary, these are set out in square brackets exactly as they are in the 'Sizes' section of the pattern.

MATERIALS

To allow you the greatest possible scope for experiment in these patterns, we have chosen to specify only general types of yarn, rather than specific qualities or brand names. However, for those who wish to knit a colourway similar to the one in the photograph, we have given general descriptions of the colours used (or you can send for a kit, see page 143). As long as it can be knitted up to the correct tension, you can use any suitable four-ply, or double knitting or whatever (this means that, to be on the safe side you should make a tension check with one ball before buying enough yarn for the whole garment). In most cases, we have also specified the overall yarn type used for a particular design, for example, 'four-ply wool' or 'four-ply cotton'. This does not mean that you cannot knit up the sweater in another type of yarn, but if you do, you must be careful about the yarn quantities. Cotton is heavier than wool so it takes more cotton (in terms of weight) to knit up the same garment than it does wool. You will need to buy a few extra balls of the main colour, if you are substituting cotton for wool.

In general, we use only natural fibre yarns in our work – wool, cotton, silk – and most of the time they have a smooth, non-textured finish. Many of the designs also use lots of different colours – over 20 in some cases – often in only very small quantities, so there can be lots of yarn left over. If this seems uneconomical you can use odd balls of wool from your spare yarn stock for some of the contrast colours, but only if it is a similar type and quality to the main colour.

TENSION

It is essential to check your tension before beginning to knit up a design. If the tension is not accurate, the sweater or cardigan will not be the correct size, and the yarn quantities may be inadequate. Remember that the needle size quoted at the beginning of a pattern is only a recommendation, since tension is a personal thing to the individual knitter, rather like a signature. Many, if not most, knitters will have to adjust their tension by changing the needle size.

To check your tension, knit up a sample using the yarn specified in the Materials section, and the stitch and needle size specified in the Tension section. Then count the number of stitches and rows in the sample. If there are more stitches or rows to 10cm (4in) than there should be, your sample is too tight and you should knit up another one on larger needles. If there are fewer stitches or rows to 10cm (4in) than there should be, your sample is too loose and you should knit up another one using smaller needles. Keep on adjusting the needle size until the correct tension is obtained.

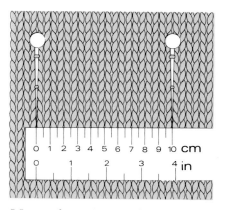

Measuring row tension
Place a ruler alongside the column of stitches as shown. Insert a pin at the zero mark and another at the 10cm (4in) mark. Count the stitches between the pins.

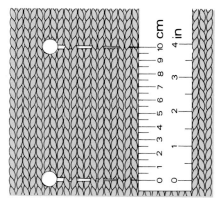

Measuring stitch tension
Place a ruler along the base of one row of stitches. Insert a pin at the zero mark and another at the 10cm (4in) mark. Count the stitches between the pins.

CHARTS

All the designs in this book are knitted from charts where one square on the chart is the equivalent of one stitch of knitting. Each square is given a particular symbol denoting the colour used to work the stitch, or there may be a code number covering a group of stitches of the same colour. Unless otherwise indicated in the key the charts are worked entirely in stocking stitch. In most cases the knit rows are worked from right to left and the purl rows from left to right. Sometimes only the right-hand half of a chart is shown, as the left-hand is a mirror image of it. In these cases each row is worked first from right to left to the centre stitch, then from left to right over the same chart row to the beginning again.

Size markers are shown on the charts as blue lines, but where these lines indicate shaping (as in armhole or sleeve shaping) use them as a guide for placing the colour pattern only; always follow the shaping instructions written out in the pattern.

If you find it difficult to follow the design through the chart, it can be helpful to photocopy and hand-colour it. Many copying machines will also enlarge the charts if you find the squares too small.

INTARSIA

All the patterns in this book should be worked by the intarsia method. This is a particular way of handling the yarns when there are many different colours and motifs in a pattern. It should not be confused with the traditional Fair Isle method where the yarns are carried across or woven into the back of the work. The two methods produce quite different tensions and types of fabric. Fair Isle results in a double thickness, tight fabric; intarsia produces a single thickness, flexible fabric. By the intarsia method each colour area is knitted with a separate length of yarn and the different colours are twisted together at each colour join and then left in position to be used on the next row – they are *not* carried across the back.

When many colours are being worked in the same part of a garment, it can be difficult to avoid a dreadful tangle at the back of the work. If you are using smooth yarns, break off generous lengths of each colour and work with these rather than straight from the ball, then at least the loose threads can be pulled free of the tangle.

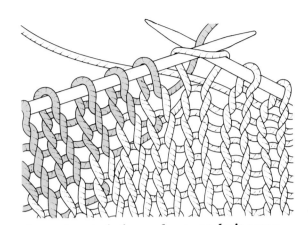

Intarsia – twisting colours on knit rows
Where a design slants to the right twist the yarns together on knit rows only as shown.

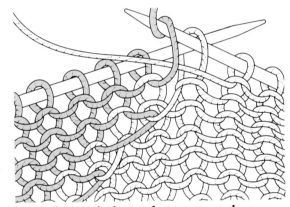

Intarsia – twisting colours on purl rows
Where a design slants to the left twist the yarns together on purl rows only as shown.

FINISHING

When many colours have been used in a design, the darning in of loose ends can be extremely laborious. If you knit them in as you go along by wrapping the ends around the main colour thread for two or three stitches beyond where they were last used, the job will be much easier. Do not cut the ends off too close to the fabric as they can work loose. Where loose ends do have to be darned in, work them neatly into the same colour area of the pattern. Block and press following the instructions on the ball band or label of the yarn. Avoid ribbed edges and textured areas such as bobbles.

Sew up using backstitch seams for joins which run parallel with rows (like shoulder seams). Invisible seams are ideal for joining pieces of stocking stitch where the join runs at right angles to rows (such as side seams).

Because of the danger of colours running, all our garments should be dry-cleaned.

HINTS FOR AMERICAN KNITTERS

American knitters will have few problems in working from English patterns and *vice versa*. The following tables and glossaries should prove useful.

TERMINOLOGY

UK	US
cast off	bind off
catch down	tack down
stocking stitch	stockinette stitch
Swiss darning	duplicate stitch
tension	gauge

All other terms are the same in both countries.

YARN EQUIVALENTS

The following table shows the approximate yarn equivalents in terms of thickness. However, it is always essential to check the tension of substitute yarns before buying enough for the whole garment.

UK	US
Four-ply	Sport
Double knitting	Knitting worsted
Aran-weight	Fisherman

NEEDLE SIZE CONVERSION TABLES

The needle sizes given in the patterns are recommended starting points for making tension samples. The needle size actually used should be that on which the stated tension is obtained.

Metric	US	Old UK
2mm	0	14
2¼mm	1	13
2½mm		
2¾mm	2	12
3mm		11
3¼mm	3	10
3½mm	4	
3¾mm	5	9
4mm	6	8
4½mm	7	7
5mm	8	6
5½mm	9	5
6mm	10	4
6½mm	10½	3
7mm		2
7½mm		1
8mm	11	0
9mm	13	00
10mm	15	000

METRIC CONVERSION TABLES

Length
(to the nearest ¼in)

Weight
(rounded up to the nearest ¼oz)

cm	in	cm	in	g	oz
1	½	55	21¾	25	1
2	¾	60	23½	50	2
3	1¼	65	25½	100	3¾
4	1½	70	27½	150	5½
5	2	75	29½	200	7¼
6	2½	80	31½	250	9
7	2¾	85	33½	300	10¾
8	3	90	35½	350	12½
9	3½	95	37½	400	14¼
10	4	100	39½	450	16
11	4¼	110	43½	500	17¾
12	4¾	120	47	550	19½
13	5	130	51¼	600	21¼
14	5½	140	55	650	23
15	6	150	59	700	24¾
16	6¼	160	63	750	26½
17	6¾	170	67	800	28¼
18	7	180	70¾	850	30
19	7½	190	74¾	900	31¾
20	8	200	78¾	950	33¾
25	9¾	210	82¾	1000	35½
30	11¾	220	86½	1200	42¼
35	13¾	230	90½	1400	49¼
40	15¾	240	94½	1600	56½
45	17¾	250	98½	1800	63½
50	19¾	300	118	2000	70½

ABBREVIATIONS

alt – alternately
approx – approximately
beg – begin(ning)
cm – centimetre(s)
cont – continu(e)(ing)
dec – decreas(e)(ing)
foll – follow(s)(ing)
g – grams
in – inch(es)
K – knit
K up – pick up and knit
K-wise knitwise, as if to knit
make 1 – pick up loop between last stitch and next stitch and K it tbl
mm – millimetres

P – purl
patt – pattern
psso – pass slipped stitch over
p2sso – pass 2 slipped stitches over
P-wise – purlwise, as if to purl
rem – remain(s)(ing)
rep – repeat(s)
rs – right side of work
sl – slip
st(s) – stitch(es)
st st – stocking stitch (stockinette stitch)
tbl – through back of loop(s)
tog – together
ws – wrong side of work

KITS & STOCKISTS

All our designs are knitted primarily in Rowan Yarns, so although the patterns list generic types of yarn, there is a Rowan equivalent for each of the types listed. These are:

Four-ply wool – Rowan Botany
Four-ply cotton – Rowan Sea Breeze Cotton
Double knitting wool – Rowan Lightweight Double Knitting Wool
Aran-weight – Rowan Designer Double Knitting Wool

These yarns can be obtained at many of the usual stockists of good quality knitting yarns. In case of difficulty, write to the addresses below for a list of stockists in your area.

United Kingdom
Rowan Yarns, Green Lane Mill, Holmfirth, West Yorkshire HD7 1RW.
Tel 0484 687714/5/6

USA
Westminster Trading Corporation, 5 Northern Boulevard, Amherst, New Hampshire 03031.   Tel 603 886 5041

Canada
Estelle Designs and Sales Ltd, 38 Continental Place, Scarborough, Ontario. Tel 416 298 9922

Australia
Sunspun Enterprises Pty Ltd, 195 Canterbury Road, Canterbury, 3126 Victoria.   Tel 3 830 1609

West Germany
Beatrijs Sterk, Friedenstrasse 5, 3000 Hanover 1.   Tel 0511 818001

Cyprus
Litsa Christofides, Colourworks, 12 Parnithos Street, Nicosia. Tel 357 4182 1764

Denmark
Mosekonens Vaerksted, Mosevej 13, L1 Binderup, 9600 Aars.   Tel 48 8 656065

Holland
Henk and Henrietta Baukers, Dorpstraat 9, 5327 AR Hurwenen.   Tel 31 4182 1764

New Zealand
Creative Fashion Centre, PO Box 45083, Epuni Railway, Lower Hutt.   Tel 04 664 689

Norway
Jorun Sandin, Eureka, Kvakkestandgarden, 1400 Ski.   Tel 0287 1909

Japan
Diakeito Co. Ltd, 1-5-23 Nakatsu Oyodo-Ku, Osaka S36.   Tel 06 371 5653

Sweden
Eva Wincent Gelinder, Wincent, Luntmakargartan, 56 113 58 Stockholm. Tel 08 32 70 60

Yarn kits are available for all the designs in this book. Buying a kit is the best and most economical way of reproducing exactly the garment as pictured. The kits are available from three different sources.

Rowan Kits
Write to the Rowan distributors above for a list of stockists of the following designs:
Diamonds (black colourway, page 31)
Susani (cardigan only, navy colourway, page 53)
Fruits (natural colourway, pages 80/81)
Pairs (cream colourway, page 105)
Falconer (black colourway, page 115)

Ehrman Kits The following kits are available by mail order:
Sicily (black colourway, inset page 9)
Fruits (black colourway, page 84)
Garden (black colourway, pages 85 and 89)
Millefiori (fuchsia, page 133, and black colourways)

Write to the following address for details:
Hugh Ehrman, 21-22 Vicarage Gate, London W8 4AA.   Tel 01 937 4568

Seaton Kits
The remaining designs can also be obtained as kits. Write to the following address for details, enclosing a stamped addressed envelope.
Jamie and Jessi Seaton (Kit Supplies), Goetre Farmhouse, Llanfynydd, Carmarthen, Dyfed, Wales SA32 7TT. Tel 055 84 825

ACKNOWLEDGEMENTS

It's a very rare thing for anyone to achieve anything in this world without the assistance, or at least the goodwill, of a network of friends, associates and helpers. This is particularly true in our case, so it's good to have this opportunity to record in clear black and white the gratitude we feel – though lack of space dictates that this can't be anything like an exhaustive list. We can have a stab at it, at any rate.

First and foremost our thanks go to Siân Conti, our right-hand woman, whose hard work, persistence, meticulousness and good humour have been really invaluable over the last five years. Thanks also to Maureen Jones, Fran Haystead, Janet Gray and Alex Faulds – our production office gang. Special thanks to Ruth Gilbert, as steady and reliable as a rock in the treacherous waters of our lives! Thanks too to Mrs Gardner, our really excellent finisher, and her whole family. And my particular thanks to Maria Dolores Brannan, my shared assistant but very own sparring partner.

This book, too, is very much the result of a group effort. Having provided the raw material – the designs – Jess and I gratefully became no more than equal members of a very competent team. Thanks firstly to Frank Herholdt, whose wonderful photographs really provided the book with its character. Thanks to Sandy Carr for her extremely able editorship; to Marilyn Wilson for her lucid pattern writing; to Dennis Hawkins and John Hutchinson for their clear and attractive charts; and to Clare Clements for pulling it all together with her excellent layout.

Many thanks to Sue Rowlands for her inspired and sympathetic work as stylist. Aside from their expertise, Frank and Sue should be thanked for their good company, as should all who participated in our two shoots in Italy – Judith, Sandy, Dominic, Gwyn, Pennie, Bella, Thea, Stephen and Sarah – making them memorably enjoyable as well as productive times. And thanks to Sarah Wallace, our commissioning editor, who, at the same time as keeping the logistics of this and a dozen other projects clearly in mind, provided much of the creative spark that set this thing alight and kept it burning.

More generally: many thanks to Stephen Sheard for much help and encouragement over the years; and to all at Rowan Yarns for their helpfulness and openness – especially to Lyn Valentine, who occasionally comes to bear the brunt of our production crises and copes with it remarkably well! Thanks to Hugh Ehrman, both for his kit business and for his refreshingly detached perspective on the knitwear world. Thanks to Sue Jamieson for her help and hard work over many years; to Myra Hogan for the same thing in New York; and to Flavia Cappanago del Monte for her great work in Milan. Thanks to family and friends for putting up with us so valiantly for so long.

Last but not least, a huge thank you to our loyal and wonderful band of knitters, without whom none of this would really have been possible. To list a tiny sample: Anita Richards, Kath Brindle, Mrs Goon, Susan Webber, Mrs V. Reynolds, Sandra Warr, Diana Anderson, Mrs O. B. Adams, Lil Peters, Mrs Joan Thatcher, Mary Scott, Phil Smith – and five hundred more! Thank you *all* very much.

PICTURE CREDITS

Clothes and accessories were lent by the following suppliers: *Jane Bates* lent the jewellery on pages 23 and 33; *Bernstock Speirs* lent the beret on pages 17 and 21, the trilby on page 43, and the hat on page 97; *The Beauchamp Place Shop* lent the Ventilo jodhpurs on page 81; *Betty Jackson* lent the Emma Hope suede boots on page 81; *4 Eyes* lent the spectacles on pages 67, 71 and 115; *The Hat Shop* lent the hats on pages 119 and 121; *Hobbs* lent the trousers on pages 47, 121 and 124; the shoes on page 61, and the shorts on page 119; *Mary Quant Hosiery* lent the socks on pages 59 and 61; *Midas* lent the dress on pages 11 and 14, the handbag on pages 47 and 50, and the shoes on page 97; *Mulberry* lent the Écaille sunglasses on page 31, the handbag and the linen suit on page 53, the briefcase on page 59, the bag on page 61, and the belt on page 139; *The Natural Shoe Shop* lent the shoes on page 59; *Paul Smith* lent the watch on page 43, the trousers on pages 67, 71 and 89, the suit, shirt, tie and watch on page 109, and the shoes on page 115; *Viv Knowland Hats* lent the hat on page 105; *Wright & Teague* lent the jewellery on pages 1 and 133.